*The*

# HOMESCHOOL

## *Life*

### DISCOVERING GOD'S WAY
### TO FAMILY-BASED EDUCATION

# ANDREA SCHWARTZ

CHALCEDON/ROSS HOUSE BOOKS
VALLECITO, CALIFORNIA

Library of Congress Catalog Card Number: 2008902221
ISBN: 978-1-891375-50-7

*Printed in the United States of America*

For Owen,
the son of my first graduate

# QUOTES I LOVE

I am much afraid that the schools will prove the very gates of hell, unless they diligently labour in explaining the Holy Scriptures, and engraving them in the hearts of youth. I advise no one to place his child where the Scriptures do not reign paramount. Every institution in which means are not unceasingly occupied with the Word of God must be corrupt.

*- Martin Luther*

There is a brilliant child locked inside every student.

*- Marva Collins*

My heart is singing for joy this morning! A miracle has happened! The light of understanding has shone upon my little pupil's mind, and behold, all things are changed!

*- Anne Sullivan*

I learned most, not from those who taught me but from those who talked with me.

*- St. Augustine*

Education without values, as useful as it is, seems rather to make man a more clever devil.

*- C. S. Lewis*

Thank goodness I was never sent to school; it would have rubbed off some of the originality.

*- Beatrix Potter*

# TABLE OF CONTENTS

Teaching Character

Teaching Curriculum

# ACKNOWLEDGMENTS

~ to Susan Burns who graciously and kindly goes over my essays, making the necessary grammatical revisions and offering sound suggestions so that my words make sense and my meaning is clear. What would I do without you?

~ to Kathy Leonard whose efforts on behalf of this book have improved me as a writer. Someday, Kathy, I hope to meet you in person.

~ to Mark Rushdoony and Chris Ortiz of the Chalcedon Foundation who provide me with a platform to share my passion for Christian education while continuing to uphold the mission and goals of Chalcedon's founder, R.J. Rushdoony. Rush would be proud!

~ to those who read *Lessons Learned from Years of Home-schooling* and let me know how it encouraged them to "take the plunge" and begin the adventure that has changed the course of their lives. It is my sincerest hope that as they continue to home-school that they keep their eyes on Jesus, the author and finisher of our faith.

~ to my husband, Ford, and daughter Dorothy who provide me with great joy as I live out my calling as wife and mother.

To God be the glory!

# INTRODUCTION

This book, like my previous one *Lessons Learned from Years of Homeschooling*, consists of essays that first appeared as blog entries at www.StartYourHomeschool.com or as articles in *Faith for All of Life* (the magazine of the Chalcedon Foundation) and is offered to encourage and instruct those considering homeschooling or who are currently undertaking the education of their children in a homeschool setting. The essays are not presented in the order in which they were written, but have been grouped into four basic categories: Help for Parents, Teaching Character, Teaching Curriculum, Curriculum.

The need for Christian education has never been more apparent than it is in our time. Assaults on the family—the primary institution ordained by God—have multiplied at an exponential rate. Whether they are spiritual, moral, economic, educational, or in countless other areas, these attacks can only be challenged and faced with the weapons of warfare that the Bible outlines. The problem is compounded because many professing Christians have little to no idea of exactly how those weapons are to be utilized. In fact, too few Christians really comprehend the nature and extent of the war in which we are already engaged. Many still talk about the *possibility* of tribulation in the future, without recognizing that the enemy has been at our door for quite some time.

But this volume is not intended to address the reasons why Christians fail to live up to their God-given duty to raise their children in the nurture and admonition of the Lord. Rather, it is designed to encourage parents and families to embrace the victory we have in Jesus Christ and to fully embrace their part in the battle(s) before us. The song entitled "The Battle Belongs to the Lord"[1] says it quite well:

> *In heavenly armor we'll enter the land,*
> *The battle belongs to the Lord.*
> *No weapon that's fashioned against us will stand,*
> *The battle belongs to the Lord.*
>
> *And we sing glory, honor, power and strength to the Lord,*
> *We sing glory, honor, power and strength to the Lord.*
>
> *When the power of darkness comes in like a flood,*
> *The battle belongs to the Lord.*
> *He'll raise up a standard, the power of His blood,*
> *The battle belongs to the Lord.*
>
> *When your enemy presses in hard, do not fear,*
> *The battle belongs to the Lord.*
> *Take courage, my friend, your redemption is near,*
> *The battle belongs to the Lord.*

---

1. ©1985, Fairhill Music, Words and Music by Jamie Owens Collins.

# I

# The Foundation of the Christian Curriculum

Let's say you wanted to prepare an ambassador for diplomatic service. What would be involved?

For starters, you would ensure that the candidate was well versed in the ideology and practices of your country and was prepared to discuss, defend, and promote your nation's interests in the country where he was going to serve. Selections would be made on the basis of those who were in wholehearted agreement with your country's goals and purposes, and verified so as to ensure loyalty when living in that foreign culture. You would make sure that anyone sent out was additionally versed in the culture and perspectives of the destination country to be able to conduct the duties and responsibilities of the calling effectively and productively.

Aren't Christian parents charged with the same responsibility as they train their children to be ambassadors for Jesus Christ according to the Great Commission? Before we would consider sending them on such a mission, would we not need to be certain that they were well schooled in the particulars of the Christian faith as it applied to daily situations? Wouldn't we want them to be able to articulate in a coherent way what makes Jesus Christ *the Way, the Truth, and the Life?*

In other words, what would a Christian curriculum look like—one designed to impart a truly Biblical world and life view?

I've irritated more than a few people by challenging the enrollment of their children in the public school system. In fact, I'm repeatedly told by Christian pastors and elders that it is important not to be divisive on this issue. To many, it is an issue that is summed up in *agreeing to disagree.*

Their underlying presupposition is that education is a subject that the Lord has no definite opinion about. To them, attendance at church on Sundays and further participation at Sunday school or Awana clubs is all the *requisite* Christian education that children need: religious training is best handled at church, with there being no need to examine all disciplines (history, science, literature, etc.) from the Word of God.

I often challenge such folks and ask them this: as Christians, why wouldn't you send your children to a Muslim school? A Hindu school? A Mormon school? The answer: because as Christians they wouldn't want their children to be influenced against their religious beliefs! My next question: as a Christian, why are you sending your children to a *missionary* school that teaches, preaches, and mandates the state religion of humanism? As Rushdoony so ably puts it,

> A state curriculum to be true to itself must teach statism. A Christian curriculum to be true to itself must be in every respect Christian.[1]

Many professing Christians continue to enroll their children in state-run schools, thereby setting up a schizophrenic situation: Jesus Christ is professed King of kings and Lord of Lords on Sundays (and in church), but Monday through Friday, His name is forbidden to be acknowledged or even prayed to inside the walls of the state-run school where they go to be educated. In fact, often the only acceptable way to mention the name of the Lord in a public school is to take His name in vain!

---

1. R. J. Rushdoony, *The Philosophy of the Christian Curriculum* (Vallecito, CA: Ross House Books, 1981), 12.

That said, there is much more to the primary and secondary curriculum than just including the name of Jesus prior to or during the school day. Christ must be the root and branch of every subject—diffused throughout the entire course of study of history, science, literature, language, and mathematics. Children must understand that they cannot adequately comprehend the world in which they live and move apart from the Word of God as contained in the Scriptures of the Old and New Testaments. Again quoting Rushdoony:

> The sound curriculum will be the relevant curriculum, and relevancy requires two factors, a world of absolutes, and a world of change. It is not enough to hold to God's absolutes: they must be continually and freshly related to the changing times.[2]

Rushdoony used to come and lecture at my home back in the early nineties and would repeat again and again the necessity for us to view all areas of life and thought through the glasses of Scripture. For without this *vision correction*, we are doomed to both the nearsighted and farsighted distortions brought on by sin and disobedience. Through the impetus of his teaching, I came to understand that I was *personally* responsible to understand the implications of my faith in order to adequately teach and prepare my children for adulthood.

Therein lies the rub. Too many Christian parents have abdicated this role of being the primary educators of their children, passing the baton to a school system to take care of preparing their children for life and the world as adults—apart from submission to the law-word of God. In many cases, these same parents have little to no interest in becoming educated themselves with a Biblical worldview. They profess with their lips that they want children who will live and act as Christians, but with the jello-like standards of the world, almost anything qualifies. What we get is a church full of "baby Christians," at best (Heb. 5:13), and hypocrites, at worst (Matt. 7:21).

Parents must be able to discern all current events and issues of the day from a Biblical perspective. Then, should they decide

---

2. Ibid., 14.

that the best method of education is a day school rather than home-schooling their children themselves, their quest should be for a school that is committed to teaching ALL subjects from a Biblical perspective. What's more, regular "dinnertime" and "in the car" discussions should be maintained in order to evaluate the fruits of the school's teaching, not to mention the effect the values and standards of fellow students have on their children.

What follows is a non-exhaustive analysis of some of the fundamental differences between Christianity and humanism as they affect education, excerpted from Rushdoony's *Philosophy of the Christian Curriculum*.[3]

| Christianity | Humanism |
|---|---|
| 1. The sovereignty of the triune God is the starting point, and this God speaks through His infallible Word. | 1. The sovereignty of man and the state is the starting point, and it is the word of scientific, elite man which we must heed. |
| 2. We must accept God as God. He is alone Lord. | 2. Man is his own god, choosing or determining for himself what constitutes good and evil (Gen. 3:5). |
| 3. God's Word and Person is the Truth. | 3. Truth is pragmatic and existential: it is what we find works and is helpful to us. |
| 4. Education is into God's truth in every realm. | 4. Education is the self-realization and self-development of the child. |
| 5. Education is discipline under a body of truth. This body of truth grows with research and study, but truth is objective and God-given. We begin by presupposing God and His Word. | 5. Education is freedom from restraint and from any idea of truth outside of us. We are the standard, not something outside of man. |
| 6. Godly standards grade us. We must measure up to them. The teacher grades the pupil. | 6. The school and the world must measure up to the pupil's needs. The pupil grades the teacher. |
| 7. Man's will and the child's will must be broken to God's purpose. Man must be remade, reborn by God's grace. | 7. Society must be broken and remade to man's will, and the child's will is sacred. |
| 8. Man's problem is sin. Man must be recreated by God. | 8. Man's problem is society. Society must be recreated by man. |
| 9. The family is God's basic institution. | 9. The family is obsolete. The individual or the state is basic. |

---

3. Ibid., 172–173.

As is apparent from this comparison, the products (graduates) of a secular education and those of a deliberately Christian education will be radically different. What's more, these same individuals will perceive issues and ethical choices quite differently. Why should we expect the conversion of the nonbeliever when those who profess the faith more often than not share with him the same economic, political, and social premises?

We must always remember that there is a war that has been raging since the Fall of Man. Again to quote Rushdoony,

> Education is thus the power area in the modern world and the arena for the struggle between Christianity and humanism. If humanism can retain control of the schools, the logic of education will then create more and more modernism, because modernism is simply humanism in charge of the church. It will turn evangelicals into neo-evangelicals and neo-fundamentalists. It will produce, in the supposedly Bible-believing churches, a faith having the form of godliness but lacking the power thereof (2 Tim. 3:5).
>
> The recovery of the power of godliness requires a radical break therefore with humanism and humanistic education. It means that a thoroughly Biblical doctrine of education must govern the Christian school. Our hope then is not in externals and methods but in that meaning and truth which is incarnate in Jesus Christ.[4]

There is too much at stake for this continual disobedience among professing Christians to continue. All the considerations that have been used to justify and baptize the sacrificing of our children on the modern altars of Baal must be confessed and repented of. We should encourage Christian education in both the home-school and day school. If we truly want to see disciples made of all nations, we must begin in our own homes and churches.

---

4. Ibid., 161.

# Help for Parents

# 2

# A QUIET REVOLUTION

This past Saturday I participated in a homeschool forum in a nearby county. There homeschooling moms and dads spent four hours displaying textbooks and other curriculum choices they've used so they could help other families make decisions for the following school year, and answering questions about particular subjects. Unlike homeschooling conventions, there were no sales or sales pitches. The sole purpose of this gathering was for Christian homeschooling families to help one another by means of encouragement and sharing information. A number of visitors were present who were just "checking out" what this homeschooling business was all about.

Although I was the "veteran" with the longest years of service (twenty-five), there were others who displayed signs indicating nineteen, fifteen, and twelve years of homeschooling. In addition, there were those who had just begun in September of 2006. Once again I was struck with the level of commitment and congeniality that marks most homeschool gatherings. An unknowing onlooker would most likely be dumbfounded and ask questions like "What makes these people tick?" or "What's in it for them?" Of course, these are the wrong questions. The question is "Who is in them?" and the answer—the Holy Spirit.

I participated in a question and answer session over lunch. As I gazed at the faces of those in attendance, I realized just how "dangerous" a bunch we homeschoolers are! The major threat we pose to the humanistic secularism of our day is that we realize how precious a gift the fruit of the womb is—the reward we've been given—and we are actively obedient to the Giver of this gift by raising and training our children according to His holy directions.

The gates of hell will never be able to defend itself against this sort of quiet revolution. Moreover, as those of us who are veterans in this battle for the hearts and minds of our children share our experiences, insights, and *lessons learned* with those still educating their own children and encouraging other interested families to do the same, we'll be setting the stage for reclaiming our culture for the Lord Jesus Christ.

From my perspective, the day was a raving success, and I hope I get additional opportunities to attend other homeschooling forums. My biggest encouragement came from the dads who thanked me for the solidly Biblical perspective I expressed and my "unbridled passion" (as one man put it) for Christian education. I left richer—not in dollars and cents—but in the knowledge that there are multitudes of "quivers" out there across our land and the world that are being stocked by those who are learning to obey, love, and trust the Lord Jesus Christ. As a hymn we used to sing weekly during worship service renders 2 Corinthians 10:4-5,

*For the weapons of our warfare are NOT carnal, but mighty through God, to the pulling down of strongholds and casting down imaginations of every high thing that exalts itself above the knowledge of God, and bringing into captivity every thought to the obedience of Christ.*

# 3

# Lessons
# from the Cuckoo Clock

I love clocks. If you were to visit my home, you'd see all sorts of clocks in almost every room of the house. Some of these clocks chime, others ding, some play music, others have a swinging pendulum, while still others display the barometric pressure and humidity levels. The latest addition to my clock menagerie is a cuckoo clock, something I've wanted for quite some time.

Now cuckoo clocks defy modernity. This one is many years old and doesn't need batteries or electricity. Imagine that! It runs on the principle of two weights attached to a chain that allow the clock to keep time and make its cuckoo sound on the hour and half hour so long as you keep the chains pulled. One pull on each chain should keep the clock running for days.

This vintage clock was an auction item I won at the local Community Pregnancy Center fundraising dinner. It had been donated by one CPC supporter. So, when we had some difficulty making it operate correctly, we didn't have the benefit of a store to call for assistance in setting it up. Through trial and error, it eventually worked, but not before I was sure I permanently ruined it six or seven times!

The lesson here: this clock was so well made that despite my ineptitude and impatience, it works as its designer intended. A corollary lesson for homeschooling parents: your children are so well made that, despite your initial ineptitude and impatience, they can thrive and learn in the homeschooling environment, even if you are a rookie.

Many homeschooling parents feel that they might damage their children irrevocably or mar them in such a way that their futures will be forever compromised. Some even keep them in a public school setting for fear of "doing damage." However, viewed from a Biblical perspective, just the opposite is the case. Keeping them in an environment where the holy fear of the Lord is not the basis and emphasis of all subjects taught is among the most deceitful and harmful of situations thrust upon children.

Like the craftsman who produced my prize cuckoo clock, the Creator, Designer, Sustainer, and Redeemer of your children constructed His creatures (your children among them) with the capacity to withstand the bumps and mishaps from operator error!

# 4

# A Small Town in a Big City

The other night as I was an audience member for a homeschool theater production of the musical *Annie*, I was once again struck by how unique Christian homeschooling is as a cultural trend. What begins as a desire to provide a distinctively Christian education to children under the hands-on guidance and direction of the parents evolves (yes, I use that word intentionally) into a community of caring and productive families eager to serve the Lord Jesus Christ.

Guests who are not accustomed to homeschooling circles almost always remark on how well-behaved and orderly the children are, and how readily they take direction and show respect for those in authority. If you, like me, are used to such things, it doesn't seem like such a big deal. One woman, who had been a teacher in public schools and Sunday schools for over forty years, was dumbfounded that eighty plus children under the direction of about five to seven moms could be so cooperative.

After the show, people hung around to talk for twice as long as the show itself. One homeschooling mom commented, "You know, being part of the homeschooling community is like living in a small town in the midst of a big city." I was struck as to the accuracy and insight of that statement. I've been part of many groups,

15

both Christian and secular, and nothing compares to the dynamics of homeschooling families interacting with one another.

The following day I received an email that went out to the *Coram Deo Chorus* email list. Here is the text:

*Hello Dear Coram Deo Parents,*

*As we are new this year to the choir, I wanted to thank everyone for your gracious inclusion of me and my four children into your circle. My kids are thrilled to have new friends, and a place where they can grow and laugh and learn together with other homeschooled families (this is the first year I have homeschooled them). It is challenging for me at times to be the only single parent among you, but I have experienced friendship and acceptance, for which I am grateful.*

*To most of the students in the* Annie *production, it is a cute and amusing story of "rags to riches." To our family, this particular play is very close to home, since some of you know that as a single mother, I have recently adopted all four siblings. The pain of loss, the desperate desire to be loved by birth parents, the mixed blessing of adoption, the stigma of being "orphaned," and the longing to be wanted, are all realities that my children have LIVED, not just performed on a stage. It is recent pain for them, and yet they live in joy and gratitude, which is the truest miracle of God's amazing grace over them.*

*God bless you all for your efforts with your kids (and mine!). They will carry these memories forever, I am sure.*

Isn't it amazing that when parents whose primary goal and desire is to provide a daily context where their professed faith parallels their confessed faith that they that sow in tears shall reap in joy? May God be pleased to strengthen the bonds and resolve of Christian homeschooling families everywhere.

# 5

# THE HOMESCHOOL LIFE

Much has been written about the spiritual and academic benefits of homeschooling. However, one of the most significant assets of a homeschooling situation is the benefit to family life. Children often find that their best friends end up being brothers or sisters, and there is much less of a peer-group emphasis, as children of differing ages make friends with each other readily. Moreover, family outings and vacations can take place according to the family's schedule, rather than only certain periods of time during a ten-month school year.

A while back, I wrote a parody of the song from the musical *Annie*. Instead of "It's the Hard Knock Life," I changed the words to "It's the Homeschool Life." Here is my humble rendition:

*It's the homeschool life for us!*
*It's the homeschool life for us!*
*In the kitchen we learn math*
*While the baby gets a bath.*
*It's the homeschool life.*

*Siblings we always see;*
*They are classmates perpetually.*
*Who knows what grade we're in?*
*We're always with the next of kin.*
*It's the homeschool life.*

*Our moms are more than just our teachers;*
*They pile us into vans and SUVs.*
*In between the grammar, math, and science,*
*They take us to all activities.*

*No one cares that you finished all your schoolwork;*
*There is always more for you to do.*
*No relief from a parent-teacher conference,*
*Because the people who show up are you know who!*

*Oh, socialized we may not be.*
*Socialized—what's that, MTV?*
*Dad and Mom, it's thanks to you;*
*We appreciate all you do.*

*It's the homeschool life (Yes it is)*
*It's the homeschool life (Yes it is)*
*It's the homeschool life!*

All humor aside, there is an additional benefit to the homeschool life apart from academic and social aspects, and it becomes evident when there is a prolonged illness or a medical emergency in the family. These times of stress and struggle, can provide opportunities for the family to function more as God intended. Rather than become fragmented and going their separate ways, families are readily available to support and bolster each other.

I know of numerous homeschooling families in my geographical area who have had to face such medical situations. In one case, the mother of the family, after weeks of thinking she was experiencing asthma, heard the diagnosis of *Hodgkin's lymphoma*. The family of six children, the youngest eighteen months old at the time, was able to come together and act as a unit as the chemotherapy and radiation became a part of their lives for the ten week period of treatment. Did all academic subjects get covered every day? Of course not. But, now, six years later, the mom (and cancer survivor) calls the entire episode one of the great blessings in her family's life. Her children's relationship with each other and their responsibility level in the home increased greatly, as they all relied on the Lord's provision together. Academic work that was missed was made up, and if someone didn't point out this part of their history to you, you would think them an average, everyday family.

Another family is currently dealing with a father who is rapidly deteriorating from *ALS—Lou Gehrig's disease*. With the help of their church and greater homeschool community, the family has been graced to continue homeschooling, thereby giving the daughters more time with their dad to encourage him and to be around to help their mom. But, you may ask, *aren't their academics suffering?* I submit that what they are learning in a "real life" setting about illness, medical care, compassion, and God's provision, along with the studies that they are able to keep up with, will serve them profitably in the days and years ahead. They are definitely not missing out, when you consider that their appreciation for even the small blessings in life are marks of their greater maturity. Plus, they are seeing firsthand the committed bond of love between their parents—even in the face of such a brutal disease.

Yes, the homeschool life is a working model of the Biblical family. It allows families to live, learn, and work together in a full-orbed, non-compartmentalized existence. Isn't it just like our God to reward Biblical responsibility in such a beautiful way!

# 6

# GIANTS IN THE LAND

One of the continuing benefits of being a homeschooling parent is that you get to relearn things you should know over and over again as you introduce new subjects to your students. This is especially true of the excellent practice of reading passages from Scripture aloud to your children. Presenting the text with expression, thereby making its meaning come alive, followed with discussion about how the attitudes and perspectives of the people toward God affected their situation, reinforces the truths of Scripture to the one reading as much as to those listening. However, I've found that I can be quite uppity at times regarding my "ancestors in the faith" as I critique their moves and motives as though I would have done a better job! How many times have I screamed at the patriarch Isaac about choosing the ungodly son over the one God had told Rebekah would rule over the older? I hate to see him make that error time and again! And what about David? I mean, doesn't he see what effect his heinous sin is going to have on his descendants? Reading these "family histories" can act as a valuable reminder that we are very much like (if not worse) than those who've come before us.

Numbers 13 and 14 is another good case in point. In that account, Moses had sent twelve spies into Canaan to spy out the land that the Lord had promised them for a possession. Ten of the twelve came back having drawn the conclusion that they wouldn't be able to prevail against the giants in the land. Their solution was to walk by sight, not by faith. In a similar way, many Christian parents today, when they are plotting a course of action for their children's "higher education," have their gaze more fixed on the giants in the land than on the provisions and promises of the God of Scripture. In fact, they believe that if they don't have enough "AP" (Advanced Placement) courses, or letters of recommendation, or a high enough GPA from an "accredited" school, that they won't be able to get into the "best" colleges. Since their focus is on the wrong things, instead of making sure their children are strongly grounded in a Biblical world and life view and are living out the implications of their faith, they are busy spending oodles of time and money trying to get the best situation that the "giants in the land" will deem worthy.

Need I remind all of those who have bought into this philosophy that for the Children of Israel, this resulted in a total of forty years of wilderness wanderings? Come to think of it, I can't think of a better way to describe many professing Christians I know who, after having graduated from those "best" schools, end up thinking and acting much like the heathens who run them, while wandering in a wilderness of their own making. When they "mature" into adulthood, their decisions and perspectives are more "Canaanite" than they are Christian.

I am truly saddened that there is no quick fix for this attitudinal malaise. However, I am encouraged that there are many who correctly discern the war raging against the Christian faith all around them, and yet continue to persevere in the process of raising warriors obedient to the law-word of Jesus Christ. Our victorious hope lies in the reality that by focusing on the promises rather than the problems, the land will be ours!

# 7

# SPEAKING INTO THEIR LIVES

There is a time in everyone's life when the realization comes into full view that one's parents are not without flaw. It is unnerving to learn that those people who you were sure knew everything and could make all boo-boos better had shortcomings and areas of sin in their own lives. The next shock comes when after years of dismissing their concerns and admonitions, and you become a parent yourself, that you realize that your mom and dad were wiser than you imagined when it came to the important issues of life. Then, you get a little break from reality as you bask in the glow of having a little one who is sure you know everything about everything and can make all things better, only to be rudely awakened when those same fans turn into critics, pointing out your failings and limitations.

The reality of living out these various stages in family life can be exhausting and anxiety-filled as children grow into young adults—testing the boundaries of acceptable behavior, while reminding parents of their observable deficiencies and inadequacies. Having experienced all this firsthand (both as a child and parent), and witnessing this phenomenon in the lives of other homeschooling families, I've come to the conclusion that we don't have enough *aunts* and *uncles* in the Body of Christ. I see a tremendous

23

need for the greater body to establish the sort of relationships that develop in extended families. I'm suggesting that rather than being uninvolved spectators when we see Satan and worldly allurements wreaking havoc in the homes of Christian families we know, that we become active participants, walking alongside both parents and children, offering them support and encouragement. Providing an "outside" voice, which reaffirms the Word of God, is a practical out-working of St. Paul's instruction in the book of Galatians to "bear one another's burdens" and "to do good unto all men especially unto those of the household of faith" (Galatians 6:1–2, 10).

For example, let's say you become aware that a family in your Christian circle is dealing with dress issues regarding their daughters. Rather than merely sitting back and remembering the *bad old days* when you had those makeup, fashion, or dating struggles yourself, you make it a point to caringly insert yourself into the life of that family, relating to the girls by demonstrating real interest in their lives. Just as a biological aunt wouldn't be put off by a less-than-smooth initial contact, neither should the spiritual aunt if this relationship takes time to develop. Once it has been established, you can *courageously* speak into the lives of these young women, imparting the wisdom that you've acquired from your own Christian walk and lifetime of experience. Sharing stories from your own past, while refraining from lecturing, along with ongoing informal discussions, lends support to whatever their folks are trying to address with them (James 5:19–20). It also lets them know that whatever struggles they are experiencing aren't unique to them.

My point is that often young people will "hear it" from an outsider—someone not actively engaged in the struggle—rather than from their parents, and will hopefully take to heart what you've shared. By upholding the standards they're being taught at home, you'll find sincere gratitude from their folks for your "bearing this burden" with them. What's more, a little love and encouragement from others can do a world of good and help prevent situations from developing into crises.

I intentionally used the word *courageous* earlier because there is that distinct possibility that your efforts won't be welcomed or received in the spirit in which you offered them. But, like all other commands in Scripture, it is more important to obey God than worry about being personally rejected. Invest in a young person today; the Body of Christ will be stronger for it.

# 8

# RETHINKING EDUCATION

Should the process of becoming an educated person be stressful? Should students feel "pressure" when it comes to learning? By what standard should graduates be deemed ready for the adult world?

Having been a home educator for almost half of my life, I have had the benefit of selecting my own curriculum and setting my own time schedule for learning. I knew, through research, what was ahead for my children and organized my course of study for them so that they would be ready for entrance into the next stage of their education. Sometimes the journey was smoother than others. As time went on, I made it a policy and priority of our homeschool that moving on to the next level of a subject would occur only when the previous level had been mastered. This sometimes meant that my student was still doing fifth-grade-level math when she was in her seventh grade. So what? What mattered was that she understood and could apply the material, not how long or exactly when she understood it. Our culture puts a greater emphasis on when something is grasped, rather than if it is truly comprehended. (I often make the analogous observation that most adults when they interact with each other don't really care at what age the other was toilet trained; they are just gratified that they are!

27

Yet, mothers "stress" over this milestone, as though any delay will have catastrophic consequences. I wonder how often this is fueled by the desire to enroll their little ones into a daycare situation.)

It is not unusual to see high school students develop ulcers because of all their homework, AP classes, and the "need" to succeed. Many become obsessed in their quest to achieve high SAT scores and gain acceptance into the "best" universities. However, they often don't have a clue as to how to offer a good apologetic for their Christian faith, and they are altogether ignorant of church history. This isn't that surprising because their parents usually are in the same boat. What we end up with are Christian people who know much more about the *world* than they do about their *faith*. It should come as no surprise then, when faced with decisions of whom to elect to political office or which policies should be implemented and those that should be countered, that they don't have a Biblical orientation point from which to proceed. Thus, we get "business as usual," despite the fact that we live in a country with so many *professing* Christians who claim to believe the Bible from cover to cover!

Why have we allowed learning to be hijacked by the humanistic concept that grades determine a person's capabilities and that getting into the "right" school serves as a measure of personal worth? The Scriptures instruct us to seek first God's Kingdom and righteousness, and then all that we require will be added unto us. It would appear that many have accepted a counterfeit answer to the question, What should I do with my life?

The missing ingredient in all this is a lack of understanding of *calling*. What exactly is calling? Simply put, one's calling is the particular way the Lord has chosen for each individual to personally glorify and enjoy Him forever. In that vein, it is vital that young people get a chance to develop according to their giftings and inclinations within a context of self-conscious Christian education. In the process of becoming educated, stress and anxiety need not be the norm, nor sleepless nights and caffeine-filled days.

Psalm 127:1–2 asserts:

*Except the LORD build the house, they labour in vain that build it: except the LORD keep the city, the watchman waketh but in vain.*
*It is vain for you to rise up early, to sit up late, to eat the bread of sorrows: for so he giveth his beloved sleep.*

What would a society look like where the focus of young people wasn't centered in their school, but in and with their family as they make their preparation for usefulness as adults? Home-schooling gives us a microcosmic glimpse. Even so, isn't it time that we RETHINK the particulars of education?

# 9

# Recovery Mode

One of the best parts about being really sick is the opportunity to reevaluate "health" from the perspective of its opposite. This past week, I had this chance as my body succumbed to "that flu that is going around," and my days involved periods of being asleep and periods of wishing I was asleep. During this time, unable to proceed with all the things that "had to get done," I realized afresh that the world continues to spin without me watching over it. Additionally, the care and concern of my husband was decidedly evident, as was the flexibility that home education allows under such circumstances.

My homeschooling student graciously caught the flu at the same time I did, and we were both "sickies" together. "Oh," you say, "you must have lost a lot of school time." But the truth of the matter is that we were able to shift our focus from our normal routine and found opportunities to use the faculties we had at our disposal (ability to watch and hear things) and used the DVDs graciously brought in by my husband/nurse. Whether we were viewing a documentary, an educational video, or just a movie, each gave us the opportunity to discuss things like Biblical worldviews in modern depictions of life and living.

With chicken soup in hand, vaporizers going, and tissue boxes strewn throughout the room, we were able to discuss things like, What perspective do the main characters have regarding God and law? How do the characters identify and solve their problems? Was the truth about sin revealed or were transgressions whitewashed, or worse, exalted? Although no threat of testing or papers to write accompanied these excursions into learning, learning was indeed taking place.

I cannot stress enough the necessity for the homeschool curriculum to be infused and saturated with a thoroughly Biblical worldview that instills the premise that God's Word speaks to every area of life and thought. Then, even when a "break" from the normal is necessary, the time can still be redeemed in a God-honoring and productive fashion.

# 10

# I'd Be Lyin' If I Didn't Tell You about the Lion

It is easy to assume that if you homeschool your kids, teaching them all things from a faithfully Biblical point of view, everyone will live happily ever after and they will grow up actively serving and praising the Lord. As many who've traveled this path before can tell you, that just isn't always the case. Sometimes they stray from the path you've guided them on and there is much heartache that ensues. God instructs us, though, to be faithful and states that He will determine the results. That's why homeschooling would be an impossibly insane activity without receiving and living by the doctrine of the Sovereignty of God. Not only does the Lord promise that His purposes will be accomplished, He walks beside us to comfort us on our journey.

> Come unto me, all ye that labour and are heavy laden, and I will give you rest. Take my yoke upon you, and learn of me; for I am meek and lowly in heart: and ye shall find rest unto your souls. For my yoke is easy, and my burden is light. (Matt. 11:28–30)

Without this undergirding, I seriously doubt that I would be an active home educator after twenty-five years and still eager and ready to help those just starting out.

Along with this portion of Scripture, there is a warning in 1 Peter 5:8 that we need to heed for ourselves and alert our children about: the ever-present reality of the battle for their souls.

*Be sober, be vigilant; because your adversary the devil, as a roaring lion, walketh about, seeking whom he may devour.*

This enemy waits for openings, and if the homeschooling parent allows ungodly, disrespectful attitudes to go by unchallenged, that roaring lion is ever-ready to come in and encourage these and other sins against God. But, even if all things are done by the *Book*, there is still the reality that some children consummately reject the teachings of their parents and walk in paths they've been warned against. However difficult it is to accept, we don't make Christians; the Holy Spirit does.

Lest anyone be faint of heart and determine that this homeschooling task is beyond his capabilities, let me remind you of another Lion referenced in Revelation 5:5. This is He who is the King of kings and Lord of lords. The same One who came to earth to do for us what we were unable to do for ourselves. If He was capable and ready to redeem us from sin, will He not also be with us as we labor for the hearts and souls of our children? You see, I'd be lyin' if I didn't tell you about this other Lion!

# II

# GUILT BY ASSOCIATION

I'm not much for network TV. In fact, I avoid it at all opportunities. However, recently I overheard a segment of a "lawyer show." In it a "well-meaning" aunt was trying to get legal custody of her two nieces who, in her opinion, were not being raised and reared properly. The major problem was that the children were homeschooled and very much influenced by their parents' prejudicial views.

Interestingly enough, the show was not unwilling to extol the academic benefits and opportunities available to homeschooled children. One portion had one of the two girls pointing out how academically challenging her course work was. She was adamant that she loved being taught by her folks and appreciated being able to move at an accelerated pace. But, by making this unsympathetic, white-supremist family the representative of all those who homeschool, they were in effect nullifying these well-documented benefits, by demonstrating the "heinous cost" of allowing parents to make educational decisions without government supervision. The audience was to conclude that there is a huge cost to a society that allows parents to have such a major input into their children's lives.

In the end, the parents retained custody of their children. However, not unlike the skewed account of the Scopes Trial in the

35

movie *Inherit the Wind*, the audience was supposed to be repulsed by the fact that homeschooled children were systematically prevented from learning tolerance and an acceptance of all people—attitudes that would be cultivated under the auspices of state-controlled education.

How should we respond to such a smear campaign masquerading as drama? Should we protest? Boycott sponsors? No, I submit that we should keep doing what we have been doing and are commanded to do: *Train up our children in the nurture and admonition of the Lord.* That is what has got these folks bothered in the first place—the fact that our children are learning the Word of God and applying it to all aspects of their lives, emulating the Savior Jesus Christ. Recall that *He* has always been the most offensive part of Christianity! But, those that hate Christ know they cannot accomplish their desired ends by launching a blatant, frontal attack. So, instead, they malign thousands of homeschooling families by associating them with white supremists—clearly a propaganda ploy—setting up convenient straw men of Hollywood's fabrication.

Taking a look at the big picture, it tells me that our enemies are scared. After all, as my husband likes to say, *No one kicks a dead dog.* I guess the life that is exuding out of the homeschooling movement alarms them. We must take comfort in the words of Scripture that tell us that *greater is He that is in us than he that is in the world!* And, as we go about living our lives and interacting with the culture around us—shining our light before men and pointing them to our Father in heaven—we will be able to convey an accurate picture of what Christian homeschooling is all about and the good citizens it produces.

# 12

# FATHERS

I suspect that if most homeschools are like mine, the mother in the household is responsible for most of the actual teaching. There are exceptions, of course, but I would say that this is true most of the time, especially because homeschooling families with stay-at-home moms often rely primarily on one income. So, it would be easy to suppose that fathers are by-and-large irrelevant when it comes to the day-in and day-out success of academic work. *Wrong conclusion.* Without the father's role being filled (either by the dad himself, or a godly substitute in the case of widowhood or divorce), the result looks more like a tug-of-war than education.

To make an architectural analogy: in the structure of the homeschool, the Word of God is the foundation, the father assumes the role of the roof and walls, and the mother handles most of the interior decoration and arrangement. Without the covering of the father/husband there isn't much to decorate or arrange. The storms of life (*nicely provided by the world, the flesh, and the devil, not to mention those problems sent by God to further our sanctification*) are weathered by a strong outer structure so that those in the interior stay dry and safe.

To be sure, when it comes to the academic or business success of my older children, I am often credited with having given them a good foundation. And this is true. But, what remains largely unheralded and overlooked is that without my husband supporting and encouraging the entire enterprise, the fruit wouldn't be as good, and I would most likely be called a "former homeschooling mom" rather than the active one I am today.

All this being said, it is vital for the husband/father in the homeschool to be an expert when it comes to God's law-word and its application to his family. Over the years, many a dispute that has arisen between my children/students and me has been astutely handled by my husband's patient listening, followed by insightful comments that, more often than not, open the door to resolution. These were not whimsical solutions, but ones where God's enscriptured Word was given prominence and authority.

Lastly, I would be remiss in failing to acknowledge a bit of envy that often permeates my soul when it comes to my husband dealing with our children. From the time they were very little, the deep sound of Daddy's voice was something that produced immediate change that mine never seemed to accomplish. I've always wanted that deep, male voice when it comes to getting results or altered behavior in the kids. And this phenomenon didn't change when they got older. Even as some were *feeling their oats*, nothing brought them back down to earth faster than the God-given authority of their earthly father using his "get your attention" voice.

So, here's a round of applause for all the thousands of homeschooling dads who propel one of the most significant movements in our time—one that is sure to realize the furtherance of the Kingdom of God on earth!

# 13

# FILLING THE GAP

In an earlier essay, I spoke about the vital function that fathers play in the success of homeschooling. I knew that I would need to address the concept of selecting a godly "substitute" in the case of women who were widowed, divorced, or who had never been married. Here are my thoughts on this subject.

First of all, the role that is to be replaced as far as the homeschool is concerned is *father*, not *husband*. This is an important distinction. I'm not saying that a woman cannot successfully homeschool if she is not married. Sure, a two-parent household is ideal, but just as a person can continue to live a productive life with one kidney, one leg, or one eye, etc., so too can a homeschool succeed with just one parent. As the person who has lost a vital part of his anatomy needs to make adjustments or get aids to help in dealing with the loss, so too does the homeschooling mother need some assistance when dealing with the discipline of her children.

Grandfathers, uncles, and older adult brothers can function in this capacity. There must be a consensus of what the standards and rules are, and an agreement that the surrogate will act in accordance with, not in opposition to, the mother. In the absence of blood relatives, an elder, deacon, or member of the church might be willing to take on such a commitment. And a commitment it is.

For this is a role that will continue until the homeschooled child reaches a point where he is ready to make significant lifetime choices and live them out.

The covering and protection of the father-figure can be aided by members of his immediate family. In the case of a nonfamily member taking on this responsibility, he must have the support and assistance of his wife in making this a family ministry. Showing up for important events and providing encouragement for the milestones of life can be a shared activity with his own family. Care must be taken that no improper bond or relationship develops between the father figure and the mother without a husband. The man's role in this is to fill the "father gap," not to become a substitute for the love and care the single, divorced, or widowed woman may desire.

The Body of Christ is a family. Galatians tells us to "Do good unto all men, especially unto them who are of the household of faith." This is a tangible way for church members to make a huge difference in the lives of fatherless children.

# 14

# FAITHFUL ARE THE WORDS OF MY FRIEND

I have a most faithful friend whom I have known for over twenty years. During that time, I have only had the pleasure of sharing time with her in person on two occasions. Yet, this friend has been there for me in some of the most intense and important experiences of my life, not to mention times of sweet fellowship that I have enjoyed with other believers. Most recently her words provided the very real comfort I needed during an episode of sorrow. Words I have listened to for over fifteen years were used by God to convict and encourage me during a moment of overwhelming doubt. And yet, this friend is not very original in what she has to say. In fact, she constantly uses Another's ideas and words to make her point. You might say that she rarely has an original thought.

If you haven't already heard of her, I would like to introduce you to my very good friend. Her name is Judy Rogers, and she is a songwriter who has produced a body of musical work that is geared to support and encourage the Christian individual and family to stand firm in the faith of the Father, Son, and Holy Spirit. You can get a great sampling of her CD offerings by visiting her website (www.judyrogers.com). Here is some background on this godly woman:

Judy was born and raised in the Appalachian Mountains of southwestern Virginia. Her parents are dedicated Christians who taught their children the love and fear of our great God. Her dad is blessed to be very musical, and her mom is a wonderful writer of stories, poems, and songs. These gifts were present in all four of their children, and they have all sought to use them for the Kingdom of Christ.

Judy has been married to Wayne Rogers, a pastor, for thirty-eight years. Their three children were the greatest reasons Judy began writing songs in the early 1980s. Believing that music is powerful and that children can learn much more than we often give them credit for, Judy began writing songs that were distinctively Biblical, thought provoking, and melodically addicting! Wayne suggested that Judy write songs for the major themes of the Westminster Children's and Shorter Catechisms and, as they say, the rest is history.

Judy's music continues to minister to me even after years and years of having it accompany me in my car, at the gym, and even through my twenty-five years of homeschooling. In fact, my two youngest children could sing the Ten Commandments and the Lord's Prayer long before they could recite them, thanks to her first recording *Why Can't I See God?* And this is a great comfort to me, knowing that the Word of God was planted and watered within them with the help of resources like Judy's music.

No, Christian education (whether through homeschooling or Christian schools) doesn't guarantee that there are no bumps, bruises, and detours along the way for our children. But, with a firm foundation laid in God's law-word and with the help of moms like Judy Rogers, God has given us the weapons of our warfare!

# 15

# EXPERTS

What exactly makes someone an expert? Are the criteria objective or subjective? By what standard does someone earn this designation?

This past weekend while participating in a gathering of homeschooling families, I was deemed an expert because of my "twenty-five years of service." Another woman who had been homeschooling for almost two decades told me, "You're one of the sage women like me." We both agreed that we had earned every one of the gray hairs on our heads! To these homeschooling families, my longevity at this particular endeavor meant that they should give attention to what I had to say.

Today, while at the athletic club, I overheard two women discussing another woman who was a gifted musician and worship leader at their church. They each couldn't say enough good things about her, with one exception. They were dismayed because she hadn't finished her degree. One added, "If she would just go back and get her degree, she could be a wonderful music therapist." The other agreed that this would complete the package for this gal. Forget the fact that each of them had firsthand experience of her capabilities both with music and with children. For them, she needed to get credentials.

Too many parents who wish to provide a Christian education and establish homeschools are "put off" by similar considerations. They are sure that they don't have the ability to educate their children. This would be understandable if they weren't educated people—but many of them are. They have a strong commitment to the Bible and its application in their lives. But, they have been duped into thinking that it takes an "expert" to teach a child to read and compute.

I maintain that anyone who can read or compute, with a bit of encouragement and orientation to correct methods (phonics for reading and memorized and practiced drills for arithmetic), can produce students with high levels of achievement. How do I know this? Because I've done it with my own children and have witnessed it with countless others. Surely there are those who choose to delegate this responsibility to others, but it is a ridiculous statement to assert that it takes twelve years of high school, four years of college, and another year or two for a master's degree in order to teach one's own language to a young person. Anyone interested in purchasing some swampland, too?

Make no mistake about it: homeschooling isn't a mindless activity that anyone can undertake. In fact, if it is not pursued in a godly, systematic fashion, homeschooling can end up being just another way to be irresponsible. Homeschooling parents need to be pursuing a study of the Word of God with an eye to its authority over and application to all disciplines: academics, the arts, and even choices of athletics and recreation. The good news is that it doesn't take years and years of training before one can begin. On-the-job training is a very workable system, especially with all the mentoring and guidance help of curriculum publishers and other veteran "experts" like me.

I submit that homeschooling moms are among the most educated (in the truest meaning of the word) of teachers. How many other "professionals" take students from beginning to end and are versed in all the subjects in between? So, rather than deferring to so-called experts, I challenge any who are being led by the Holy Spirit to provide a home education for their children, to become an *expert* in the eyes of the Lord.

# 16

# ... AND ON THOSE BAD DAYS?

Y es, we all have them. Those days when we're sure that nothing else could possibly go wrong, and then we surprise ourselves. Expressions like *throwing in the towel*, *bailing out*, and *running away from home* all float through one's mind. What to do on such days?

Within the ranks of Christian women I know, there are those I can call upon in such times of distress who "won't let me off the hook." These are women whom I trust to be real with me when I am in a state of frustration and despair. Why have these women earned my trust? Well, for starters, they don't have me up on a pedestal. To them, I'm just who I am, and they don't have some unrealistic expectation that says, "Nothing must ever go wrong at her house!" Moreover, they know the details of my life and situation and aren't reluctant to point out that I'm whining or rehashing issues that I need to turn over to the Lord. Some of these "counselors" of mine don't even live in my state, nor do we get to see each other in person very often due to the distance between our homes. That said, they are among my dearest and closest sisters in Christ.

I recommend that all homeschooling moms have a "short list" of other women to whom they can repair and grant permission to speak directly into their lives. But these selections should not be made frivolously. Make sure that the person you summon for help will be the sort of person who uses the Word of God to counsel and uses it in an orthodox way. She should be ready and willing to exhort you rather than merely commiserate with you. If she is a decade or two older, that is a bonus! Most likely she'll have the benefit of a long-range perspective that gives her insight as to how dire your circumstance actually is. Chances are you'll leave these conversations with a smile, having reevaluated your problem with a plan to work out whatever the difficulty was. Additionally, you'll have another opportunity to praise God for the sister He has provided for you!

# 17

# This Wasn't
# on My Agenda Today

It's a funny thing that circumstances you deem problematic at one point in your life turn out to be among the most helpful. Take for example the common circumstance within a homeschool setting whereby "things happen" that aren't on your agenda for a particular day, forcing an upheaval in the daily schedule. For me, yesterday counted as one of those days.

It was midmorning, and we had already covered our Bible study, learned and went over thirteen new vocabulary words (SAT type prep), and were well into the math portion of our morning. While my student was tackling some algebra problems, I thought I would finish up some laundry that I had begun the day before. Little did I know that since the last time I was in the laundry room, the liquid soap container had fallen and broken. So as I made my way to "make good use of my time," I encountered a very slippery, soapy floor, nearly falling down.

Now I mention all this because this mini-crisis needed immediate attention, and I needed the help of my daughter. Thus, algebra stopped for a while, and she got me some towels so that I could clean up the spill and not injure myself in the process. Years ago, circumstances like this brought on tremendous anxiety. "But I can't handle this now! This is school time. If my kids were in a

47

regular day school, they wouldn't be called upon to help clean up messes!" Yes, I was guilty of trying to make my homeschool just like a day school. Either I'd handle these sorts of problems myself while my children "kept working on their studies," or I'd feel as though I was breaking some cardinal rule or law by having them stop and help me.

What's changed? For one thing, I've traveled this road before with two older children and I'm better aware of where I'm headed. But mostly, I've learned that it is in the midst of the unplanned situations and problems of life that much learning and discipling opportunities occur. My daughter had to learn yesterday that some things take priority over others. Her math lesson would keep, but an unsafe situation in the laundry room had to be taken care of. She also learned that part and parcel of keeping and managing a household involves being flexible and solution-oriented despite how trivial or unpleasant an issue appears. I think the reason that moms in general and homeschool moms in particular can multitask as well as anyone is because they have to stay on target throughout the day in the midst of changing circumstances.

By the end of the day my laundry room floor was pristine, the algebra problems were corrected, and only one subject needed to be rescheduled for the following day. But, the piano lesson still took place, I made it to my board meeting on time, and dinner made it onto the table (albeit a bit late). And, as it turns out, we'll have more time today, because the homeschool mom who helps my daughter with her biology lab called needing to reschedule their weekly time together because of a necessary, unexpected change in her agenda.

I'm hoping that no matter what academic credentials my daughter acquires at the end of her name after she's completed her education, that she will also have the confidence that she can manage a household and deal with the little things of life and take them in stride. The words of Jesus come to mind, "Well done, good and faithful servant; thou hast been faithful over a few things, I will make thee ruler over many things" (Matt. 25:23).

# TEACHING CHARACTER

# 18

# STANDING ON
# YOUR OWN TWO FEET

Is the goal of homeschooling to produce graduates who are self-sufficient and able to independently stand on their own two feet? I must confess that there was a time when I held that position and worked toward that end as a homeschooling parent/teacher. However, I have come to the conclusion that this sort of thinking is unbiblical and very humanistic.

The problem that Adam and Eve had in the garden was their delusional assumption that they COULD be self-sufficient and act independently from God. Not only were they disabused of this wrong notion when they were escorted out of Eden, but they conveyed this aberration to their posterity in the form of original sin. All successive generations have been born laboring under the delusion that they can be as God, determining for themselves what is right and what is wrong.

Our humanistic culture exalts the self-made man, the independent thinker, the "I can do it all by myself" attitude. Our fictional heroes are those who excel by lifting themselves out of the mire of common life, taking on the world single-handedly against all odds, thereby becoming heroes to those around them.

Jesus told his disciples that they needed to receive the Kingdom as a child. As any parent knows, children come out of the shoot very dependent individuals who need constant care and direction. As we apply outside discipline to their lives, we should be training them to be self-disciplined—not self-sufficient. As they mature under our care and upbringing, they should transfer the obedience to our instruction to the Lord Jesus Christ and His law-word. It is when we've conveyed this important truth and seen the evidence that they have embraced it that our full-time parenting responsibilities are complete and a mature Christian man or woman is ready to face adulthood with complete reliance on Christ.

The goal of the Christian life is one of dominion under and through the Lord Jesus Christ *in concert* with the community of fellow believers, *not* as "Lone Rangers."

# 19

# RECIPE FOR FAILURE ~ SIN IN THE CAMP

The most important aspect of Christian homeschooling is the ability to infuse all subjects with a Biblical worldview in order to provide a personal and cultural relevancy for the students. This requires a dedication to godliness that must place the love of God (the Great Commandment) above all other issues and concerns in order to have an orientation that pleases the Lord. Another beneficial aspect of the homeschooling experience is the ability for parents to focus on those areas where God has gifted or talented particular children. Whether it is in academics, athletics, the arts, or some combination thereof, special attention and suitable instruction can be tailored for the individual student. This makes the pursuit of excellence all the more possible.

Pursuing excellence and achieving excellence are two different things. For example, in cooking, one can have all the correct ingredients and the recipe still might fail if any of those ingredients are spoiled or rotten. Likewise, parents need to identify and confront the more subtle areas of sin in their children (spoiled or rotten ingredients) such as pride, ingratitude, impatience, arrogance, selfishness, insubordination, despair, laziness, rage, and blasphemy. Failing to do so may well produce a champion or an expert according to the world's standards, but hardly a suitable or acceptable ambassador for Jesus Christ.

Catechizing and instructing children from a very young age allows for easier times of correction when these attitudes and character flaws manifest themselves. Parents need to be honest with themselves and deal with their own sins in these areas by means of confession and repentance before they tackle them with their child. How blessed we are to be loved and covered by a Savior who knows our infirmities and has already paid the price. Nonetheless, we must be diligent in weeding out those aspects of striving for excellence that are self-centered and self-serving, so that we (along with our children) can fulfill our chief purpose of glorifying God and enjoying Him forever.

# 20

# QUESTIONS I CAN'T ANSWER

I think the aspect I enjoy the most as a homeschooling parent is
teaching the Bible, along with Christian doctrine and church
history. Sure, I've always attempted to present each and every subject from a Biblical perspective, but when it comes to teaching the
basic creeds, confessions, and essentials of the faith or going
through particular books of the Bible, I find that my own understanding and commitment to orthodoxy grows.

I've especially been challenged when my children have asked
questions that I could not answer. Not wanting to fudge an answer
that I am unsure about, I do some research to provide a good
response. When Dr. Rushdoony was alive, these circumstances
proved to be good excuses to phone him and chat. In fact, when his
health was failing and he acknowledged that it wouldn't be long
until he was in heaven, I lamented that he wouldn't be around to
answer my difficult questions. He laughed, "Yes, even your long
distance plan won't reach that far!" These days, I call upon the men
of Chalcedon and pose my questions to them.

I've noted the wisdom in the statement, "You know how well
a student is learning by the questions he asks rather than the
answers he gives." In fact, I would go so far as to say that as
someone is learning any subject (the Bible in particular) there

should be a host of questions that arise. Correctly applying the Scripture to life is a fundamental aspect of taking dominion in Jesus' name, and there can be no effective apologetic without it. When receiving and digesting any portion of Scripture, the obvious questions that should arise are, "How exactly does this apply to me?" and "What are the implications of this doctrine?"

Just this week my daughter posed a question that I could not easily answer. The very nature of it demonstrated to me that she is thinking through the implications of the Incarnation of Christ and His being fully God and fully man. I went to my "answer men," and they admitted that they had never considered that particular issue before. Her question got us all thinking, and the fruit of the research has given us all food for thought. How blessed I am that in the process of teaching my daughter, I am learning so very much myself!

# 21

# PRODUCTS OF OUR CULTURE

There is a huge difference between those raised in the faith and those who have not had the benefit of Christian teaching from the time they are very young. I'm reminded of a song Judy Rogers wrote, *Why Can't I See God?* The refrain goes like this:

*Teach me while my heart is tender;*
*Tell me all that I should know;*
*And through the years I will remember,*
*Wherever I may go.*

Since culture is religion externalized, there are many manifestations in our lives that reflect the culture in which we were raised. If we came to faith after childhood, there are a number of things that need to be re-thought. Often we don't think about these things until some event or circumstance brings them to our attention. For example, there are movies I loved before my conversion that, when I went to show them to my children, I discovered were not only inappropriate for them, but for me as well! It took encountering the message of the movie in *real time* before I had a chance to reevaluate it.

Once, while reading to my five-year-old daughter, this lesson was cemented. We were going through the science volume of a child's encyclopedia that I had used with her brother six years earlier, a time prior to my embracing the Reformed faith. We loved these volumes, and I couldn't wait to share them with Rachel. As I read to her from the book, we came to a section that I *dutifully* read in its entirety. The only problem was that the text was giving the earth's formation as having occurred millions and millions of years prior as the result of a "Big Bang." When we got to the end of the section, I *dutifully* informed her that as Christians we take the Biblical account of origins as correct and that this section was wrong. I then turned the page and began to read the next section. She stopped me dead in my tracks and asked in her "Rachel" style, "How do you know *this* page is *right*, when the other one was *wrong?*" She got me.

Why *was* I teaching her from a book that had incorrect, anti-Biblical presuppositions and therefore incorrect conclusions? That's when I began my "obsession" with building a homeschool library. From then on, I resolved never to use materials that weren't consistent with our Biblical faith if there were other alternatives. Where there weren't, I would teach the subject without the use of texts or books that taught lies, and present the information to my children only after I had "taught" myself.

Just the other day, I was talking with a woman who told me a story that demonstrates the sometimes unexpected benefits of raising children in the culture of the Christian homeschool. She had been reading a storybook to her five-year-old son, which began, *On Monday morning it was raining and ...* Before she could finish the sentence, he protested,

"Oh, no, Mommy! That's wrong!"

She was surprised. "What's wrong?"

"*It* isn't raining, Mommy! *God* makes it rain!"

She corrected herself, but was laughing inside. This was no small insight on the part of her Christian child—one that she had missed entirely. She realized that in this homeschooling adventure, she could expect to learn as much from her children as she would ever teach.

Homeschooling parents are positioned to raise their children with solid Biblical training. When the Word of God is presented and faithfully taught, children will reach conclusions consistent with their faith. As the Bible informs us,

*Train up a child in the way he should go, and when he is old he will not depart from it.* (Prov. 22:6)

Despite the mounting opposition we face from the humanistic culture around us the future will be bright indeed, as covenant children make their mark on the surrounding culture in Jesus' name. All the more reason for the church to *support* and *encourage* Christian homeschooling!

# 22

# OUT OF THE CLOSET

Not sure what it is about young people and the *messy room*. Or, better put, why is it that it takes me so long to do something about the hamper in my daughter's room that resembles the Tower of Babel and the "stuff" strewn on the floor that looks like the Slough of Despond? You'd think by this time I would have come up with a system to make this sort of question unnecessary.

But, you see, I thought I had. From the time my children were young, their own laundry was their responsibility, along with their own ironing. This means, of course, that they were in terrible straits when they ran out of clean or ironed clothing that was suitable for wearing. They were also responsible for seeing to it that their beds were changed regularly and that their room was dusted and vacuumed. As a homeschooling mom, I didn't have the time or energy to handle these tasks for them. Besides, I always figured it was a necessary part of growing up, to learn to take care of your own stuff. To this day, I believe my daughter-in-law appreciates that my son handles his own laundry.

In any case, this past weekend, my remaining child living at home announced to me that she was "fed up" with the condition of her room and that she was going to clean it. Now, you must understand that it isn't that big of a room. However, it has been her domain for the past fourteen and a half years and exclusively hers since 1999. Her biggest challenge was her closet, which for the past I-don't-know-how-long has teetered on an avalanche whenever she's opened the doors. It's not that she hasn't cleaned her room in years and years, but that the closet has been the recipient of anything she didn't quite know whether to save or relinquish. Throughout the day, as I was working on a number of writing projects, I was continually interrupted with yelps that went something like:

> *"I can't believe I forgot I had this doll! Remember her? I always LOVED her."*
>
> *"Look, this is my baseball glove that I got as a present when I was seven. It no longer fits! I should have used it more."*
>
> *"Can you believe this has been sitting in my closet for five years? I could still wear this hat!"*
>
> *"I think we need to give away these six pairs of shoes. I tried, but I can't even get my foot all the way in any of them."*

Periodically, I would stick my head in her room (or try to, since at times it was hard to get the door opened at all) and encourage her to shorten this stroll down memory lane and get her room to resemble more of a pleasant place to sleep than a declared disaster area. Repeatedly I needed to bring her back to the task at hand as she would bump into a memory long forgotten.

I must admit, I was extremely amused and encouraged by her response to all this. Here was my young lady enjoying the memories of her past—cherished treasures, prized gifts, trophies won, and clothes she loved. By the end of the day, many of these memories were packed up and placed for another day and time when she would revisit them. Others were put in a pile to share with others. It was as though she was identifying that childhood was a memory—a good one—but that her life now involved things more in line with her age and maturity level.

As she made her twenty or so trips to the garbage and recycling bins, she informed me that she thought she got her "pack rat" mentality from me. She kept blaming it on genetics or environmental causes. "I just find it so hard to throw anything away," she pined. Then, she came with a box and asked me what to do with some rocks. "Let me see them," I responded, figuring they were something of value that she'd been given as a present. Instead, they looked like the millions of other rocks and stones one would find in our backyard. "Why did you save these?" I asked her. "I haven't the faintest idea," she laughed back.

These are the kinds of important moments that a mother relishes spending with her daughter. In years to come, I'm sure she may not even recall this day or its events. But for me, I'm storing them in the closet of my mind where I'll be able to "dig out" memories of a day when my daughter took another full step toward womanhood.

# 23

# ON YOUR MARK, GET SET ...

How early is too early to begin homeschooling? I guess I would have to say *in utero*. After that, it is safe to get started. Seriously, people (and often medical professionals) underestimate the cognizance and awareness of infants. How often has a mom and dad glowed over the fact that their child is smiling, only to be told, "No, that's just gas." Well, I don't buy it. It's like the issue of when life begins. Any answer other than conception is grossly inadequate and flagrantly flawed. Life begins at conception, and teaching/ learning begins at birth.

Children are not blank slates. They are human beings who inherit their genes from their biological parents and their sin natures from Adam. What's more, every interaction they have from the time they are born becomes a learning experience of some sort or another. Christian parents don't serve their children in good stead when they operate as though sin isn't a real factor—one that needs to be recognized and dealt with from the outset.

Let me illustrate with two examples from my own family life:

*Case #1*

When my son was not quite a month old, we moved him out of our bedroom to sleep in his own room. He didn't like that very much and would cry and cry. Even after I did all the things a mother knows how to do, the crying wouldn't stop. This went on for some time. One night my husband had had enough of this and came into the nursery where I was leaning over the crib trying to figure out what to do. In his deep, male voice he said to our child, "Turn over and go to sleep. Your mother needs her rest." I thought to myself, *he's GOT to be kidding. This baby doesn't have the faintest idea what he is talking about.* However, I turned out to be the one who didn't have the faintest idea of what I was thinking about. Our son stopped crying immediately and went to sleep. I was dumbfounded, and my husband just trotted off to bed and went back to sleep. I had grossly underestimated the reality of a father's authority with an infant. How he knew, I can't exactly explain, but our son knew that his dad meant business.

## Case #2

My youngest daughter is fourteen years younger than her brother and seven years younger than her sister. (*I jokingly used to tell people I took a sabbatical every seven years and had a baby!*) Anyway, once when she was almost two years old, all three of the children and I were in the living room. The youngest gave her older sister a big smack in the face. I immediately slapped her hand and told her that what she had done was wrong. I then instructed her to apologize to her sister. *Nothing.* So, I slapped her hand again and told her she had done a naughty thing and needed to let her sister know that she was sorry. *Nothing.* This happened two more times. Then my son, with all the wisdom he had acquired in his sixteen years, corrected me, sure that his sister couldn't and didn't understand what I was talking about. He felt it was ridiculous for me to even imagine she could. I told him I knew she understood perfectly well, and that she was just being defiant. He rolled his eyes, certain that he was right. I reproved her again and told her to let her sister know she was sorry. *Nothing.* Again she got a hand slap. Now her sister was assuring me that the smack hadn't really hurt that badly and that Dorothy just "didn't understand." She, like her brother, wanted me to drop the whole thing. Just at that moment, my husband (ignorant of all that had transpired) walked out of our bedroom and was making his way down the hall. Dorothy didn't even see his face, just heard his steps, and very rapidly declared in a loud voice, "Sorry, Rachel!" The power of the presence of daddy had both older brother and sister dumbfounded. She *really* had understood!

I cite these examples because in each case, there was the readiness to underestimate the capacity of an infant and baby to discern right from wrong. Since the learning process has to start sometime, it might as well start immediately. So here's my short list of suggestions to begin the "pre-homeschooling" process with babies:

1. Make sure you set up a schedule that both parent and child can live with, and attempt to follow it. This applies to feeding, bathing, sleeping, and play time. Work to have relatives and friends adhere to your preferences.

2. When faced with the impatient cries of a child to be fed or changed, parents should instruct the child to calm down and then he'll be taken care of. No, it won't work immediately, but the pattern of patience will have been introduced. Parents should be consistent with this.

3. When a child is about to have a meal (nursing included) grace should be said asking the Lord to bless the food to his body.

4. When a child begins to throw a tantrum, the child should be instructed to control himself. Again, the desired response won't happen immediately, but the pattern of requiring it will be established. The child should not get what he's crying for until the tantrum is over.

5. When it is time for nap time or bedtime, the parents should vocalize to the child what they want the child to do. "It's now time to go to sleep. When you wake up, I will feed you again." Then, they should pray aloud over the child for God to bless his rest. Immediately, they should walk out of the room, close the door, and allow the child a chance to go to sleep. Again, I'm not promising immediate results, but a pattern is being laid down, that the child is expected to respect the authority of his parents.

Now, I realize that this goes against much "conventional" wisdom. I maintain that this process is actually more important for the parents than it is for the children, as the parents are the ones in charge. Holding to high standards will allow infants to grow into babies who will grow into toddlers who will grow into little boys and girls who will be able to move into an academic environment much more easily, as obedience and self-discipline have been their context from the beginning.

# 24

# OH, HOW I LOVE
# THY LAW

Life appears to be full of unanswerable questions: Why would a person go on a rampage and kill people he didn't know? Why do apparently rational people continue to pursue behaviors that are detrimental to themselves and their families? Why do people raised in the faith turn from it after years of evidence of God's blessings for obedience? And the list could go on and on.

Psalm 119 (the longest psalm in the Bible) gives us the proper focus and foundation as we face these unanswerables: *the law of God*. God's law is to be our starting point as we ponder the whys and wherefores of unexplainable events and behaviors. If God's law is not our starting point, we will be as unstable and doubleminded as unbelievers. In fact, it is safe to say that this psalm makes the benchmark of faithfulness to God synonymous with faithfulness to His law-word. An honest, careful study of this psalm establishes that the law of God *is* the delight of the believer and that he meditates in it day and night. Thus, *the* major emphasis of every Christian homeschool should be knowing, learning, and meditating on God's law and judging all things in terms of it. This constitutes the "righteous judgments" we are told to exercise in John 7:24:

*Judge not according to the appearance, but judge righteous judgment.*

By the time a person is ready to assume his role as an adult, the law of God should be so hidden in his heart that his actions, decisions, and perspectives reflect faithfulness to God's holy Word. Moreover, when called upon to give a reason for the hope that is within him, he should be able to render an answer in terms of the law-word of God. This includes being able to comment on and judge any situation or circumstance with *Thus saith the Lord* ....

Be wary of persons or teachings that elevate man's law above God's law where the two are in disagreement (capital punishment, abortion, human sexuality). Likewise, be wary of those who place their own personal opinions—their likes and dislikes—above the clear pronouncements of Scripture and justify their positions based on an "everybody knows" mentality. For example, homeschooling parents often outsource music and art instruction, along with athletic training. In cases where the parent isn't present for the lesson, it is important to "debrief" the child so that any subversive attitude or perspective does not enter in to your family unawares. Switching instructors might be in order should it become obvious that God's ways are despised or disdained.

By what standard should a godly education be judged? By ensuring that learning is taking place under the instruction of persons or a curriculum that reveres, respects, and obeys God's law and teaches others to follow it in all areas of life and thought. Of course, this means that homeschooling parents need to steep themselves in the Scriptures so that they are qualified to impart a Biblical world and life view and be able to confidently counter other perspectives that attempt to supplant and replace it. Then, when conflicts arise with modern cultural ways of thinking (and they will), and clear doctrines of the Bible are challenged by secular "truths," the words of Romans 3:3–4 will be in the forefront:

> *For what if some did not believe? shall their unbelief make the faith of God without effect?*
>
> *God forbid: yea, let God be true, but every man a liar; as it is written, That thou mightest be justified in thy sayings, and mightest overcome when thou art judged.*

# 25

# LOST IN SPACE

The year was 1984, the place was San Jose, California, and the excursion was to purchase one of those newfangled computers everyone was talking about. The unfortunate young man who was the designated salesman that night at the computer store had no idea what he was in for. The following is an accurate rendering of our dialogue:

> Salesman: May I help you?
> Me: Yes, I'm looking to buy a computer.
> Salesman: Great! What brand were you interested in?
> Me: I don't know.
> Salesman: Well, what are you going to use it for?
> Me: I don't know. What do *you* think I should use it for?
> Salesman: (*blank stare*)
> Me: Well, what do other people buy computers for?
> Salesman: Hmmmmm. I guess it depends on how they plan to use it and what features they are looking for.
> Me: That makes sense.
> Salesman: Is there something particular you want the computer to help you do?
> Me: Well, I want one of those that talks to you.
> Salesman: (*blank stare*)
> Me: You know, like they used to do on *Star Trek*? Where he would ask the computer questions, and things like that.
> Salesman: (*realizing I was serious*) Huh?

Me: Didn't you ever watch *Star Trek?*
Salesman: (*speechless and wishing his shift was over*)
Me: Well, I guess I'm not really ready to buy one.
Salesman: I think you're right. Excuse me for a bit, will you? (*never to return, and hopefully not to quit!*)

How many people approach education the same way? They know they want an education, but have no idea how they would use it. Parents can tell their children over and over again that they need to achieve good grades so that they can get into a good college, but if the student doesn't have a vision for the future, then much of the talk can fall on deaf ears.

From the time children are old enough to teach, the idea of *calling* should be a regular topic of discussion. They should understand that part and parcel of what they will end up doing with their lives will spring from where their interests lie and in what areas they demonstrate promise. Having a good idea of how they will use the acquired knowledge of studying math, history, and science should help them pursue their studies in a more purposeful way.

The first question and answer in the Westminster Shorter Catechism reads: Q. *What is the chief end of man?* A. *Man's chief end is to glorify God and enjoy Him forever.* Children should be taught that while they are young, the calling of *student* is the way in which they can glorify and enjoy their Creator. For the time spent learning of His creation, His immutable laws (both spiritual and physical), along with how He has operated throughout history will prepare the students for useful lives as adults.

The Scripture instructs us that *without vision the people perish, but happy are they which keep the law.* It is important to instill in our children the need for godly vision as they spend time preparing for the Lord's service.

(*Note: I did eventually figure out what to do with a computer!*)

# 26

# FIFTH MONARCHY MEN

Recently I had the pleasure of making the acquaintance of a young law student who is an avid Rushdoony fan and who is ready, eager, and willing to disseminate the perspectives of Christian Reconstruction. He wrote to me about the exploits he has shared with three fellow students as they unashamedly proclaim the crown rights of Jesus Christ:

> There is a very interesting story about N.D. Last semester N.D. took an appellate advocacy course in which he had to argue the Pledge of Allegiance case in front of a panel of professors. I was there for a first year review and had the opportunity to sit in on many of the sessions. Student after student provided the same historical/democratic (humanist) argument that was presented in the Pledge case. When N.D. argued the case, he challenged the court by forcing the biblical antithesis. The panel of professors was taken aback. They insisted that while his argumentation was correct from a legal and biblical perspective, he couldn't argue like that because he would only offend the Justices. N.D. pressed them to show him where his legal analysis was flawed, but they could not. In the end he was told that if he wanted to speak like the prophets of old, he would have to learn to suffer like the prophets of old. In effect he was told that the humanist sets the presupposition in the courtroom and he had been wrong for violating it. He received a much lower grade even though he had a

far superior presentation and case from a legal and biblical perspective.

We are all committed to forcing the antitheses in the legal profession and in the world. When it comes to Crown Rights of King Jesus we are all loyalists. We love to meditate on the Law of the Lord and are dedicated to seeing it lifted up as the standard in our legal system.

Here is a young man, steeped in the Biblically orthodox teaching of R. J. Rushdoony, who is willing to take a stand regardless of the consequences of those who suppose they have the power to determine his future. How prophetic were those professors comparing him to the prophets of old! As Rushdoony describes in his commentary *Thy Kingdom Come: Studies in Daniel and Revelation*, these four are Fifth Monarchy men (Daniel 2:34–35)—those who, like Daniel and his three friends, are unwilling to bow the knee to any other than the triune God of Scripture. I have run into many such young men—those ready and eager to understand how their faith translates to all areas of thinking and living. A number of them are graduating from high school this year. My present of choice: the three-volume set of *Institutes of Biblical Law* by Rushdoony. I figure it is a sound investment for the future and the Fifth Monarchy.

# 27

# CORRECTING
# YOUR CHILDREN

I'm often in mentoring situations with mothers who are eager to raise godly children, and who struggle with how well they are accomplishing this task. The question of discipline comes up regularly, and their concerns are whether they are being too strict or too lenient with their children. Over the years I've struggled with this myself, and like all other parenting issues, this is best dealt with by applying the Word of God to the issue of correction.

Everyone is born into the world with a sin nature. It is important to remember that those with a sin nature commit sins. This is where the law-word of God acts as a tutor for the child. He needs to be taught and reminded of the reality that he "naturally" is at war with God and needs a Savior so that he can come to peace with Him. Early on, children need to be taught that *sin is any want of conformity unto, or transgression of, the law of God.*

This sin nature can only be changed by an act of God through the redemption purchased by Jesus Christ and applied to an individual through the work of the Holy Spirit. We call this act of grace regeneration. However, those whose natures have been transformed through rebirth also commit sins. As parents, it is important to distinguish between those transgressions that are attempts to be obedient and miss the mark, and those that are deliberate actions carried out in defiance and/or rebellion.

When my children were young, I used the example of playing darts. The person who tries to hit the bull's-eye and misses and accidentally hits the dog is like the person who misses the mark. In the Greek, that sort of sin is *hamartia*. However, the person who is not aiming at the bull's-eye—but is rather seeing if he can hit his dog—is not missing the mark, but is aiming to miss. In the Greek, that sort of sin is *anomia*. In both cases, the dog has been hit (sin has occurred), but the motive and circumstances dictate the appropriate correction.

The analogy can help you understand which category your child's transgression falls into. The first requires that the child take responsibility for his actions by administering first aid to the dog. It also involves a time of instruction, along with establishing certain rules and procedures when dealing with sharp objects, so something like this (or worse) doesn't happen again.

In the case of the child taking sport in hurting the animal, one is dealing with a sadistic act, and discipline in the way of punishment is in order. Only after the child sees his act as sin can repentance and instruction take root.

Of course, in order to adequately apply this principle, one must not be harsher with one's children than one is with oneself. In more colloquial terms, *parents need to practice what they preach.* They cannot hold their children to a higher standard than they hold themselves. Additionally, these everyday occurrences are appropriate opportunities to share the gospel with your children as you identify where in Scripture a particular transgression is addressed (either explicitly or implicitly) and how through the blood of Jesus, one's sins are forgiven. I sometimes required an informal essay in order to cement the point with my children.

Will your emotions or personal shortcomings sometimes contribute to you applying the incorrect punishment to a given situation? Sure. What then? Well, once you assess and confess your own sin to the Lord, it is the responsible and godly thing to make things right with your children asking them for their forgiveness if you were overly harsh *or* overly lenient. That is why a systematic application of the law-word of God to every area of life and thought is so very important. Without such a standard, parents may be tempted to set up mini-dictatorships where their children have to learn how to appease the tyrant. The Biblical model is to teach children the law-word of God and make sure they understand that parents are not exempt from faithful obedience. Together, these daily course corrections will be instrumental in preparing one's children for the time they will assume responsibility for themselves and their future families.

# 28

# CALL WAITING

Today I was helping a friend—a homeschooling dad of four daughters whose speech is impaired due to ALS—make phone calls to handle financial matters and set up doctor appointments. The two hours we spent were enjoyable because Jay is one of those people to whom God has given an extra dose of funny. Sure his condition sometimes gets the better of him emotionally, but his faith in the Lord and his ability to turn the somber into laughter is something this devastating illness has not been able to touch.

When I arrived at his home, I watched his wife adroitly transfer him from his hospital bed to his wheelchair so we could get to work. We called his doctors' offices, a medical supply company, and the company that handles his employee investments. Each time I was greeted by a recorded voice directing me to punch all sorts of numbers and giving me instructions about the information needed in order to connect me to the proper person, only to have to repeat all the information over and over again. What's more, because I was acting as "Jay's mouthpiece," new permission had to be given by Jay authorizing me to speak for him to each new person who came on the line. With his diminished lung capacity, this wasn't always easy.

During the many long waits on hold listening to selections from Handel and Mozart, Jay and I commented how grateful we are that we don't have to approach the Lord this way. Just imagine how humanistic man would make the process of prayer more efficient. We figured it would go something like this:

> *Hello, you have reached heaven.*
> *Your call is important to us, so stay on the line and someone will be with you shortly.*
> *For praises, press one.*
> *For confession, press two.*
> *For thanksgiving, press three.*
> *For healing, press four.*
> *For all other petitions, please stay on the line for the next available operator.*
>
> *Please be sure to have all identifying numbers ready when your call is answered.*
> *For quality purposes, this prayer may be monitored.*
>
> *Due to heavy calling volume, there will be a significant wait. Your prayer will be answered in the order received.*
>
> (Muzak streams a synthesized version of *Amazing Wait*.)
>
> *Someone will be with you shortly. Did you know that you can bypass this call by going to our website and leaving your prayer item? Most prayers are responded to within 48 hours.*
>
> (The lovely tones of *Amazing Wait* continue!)

Eventually, real people came on the line to handle my requests for Jay, but often determined that our particular issue was not something handled by their department. I had to rehash the same account numbers and information so many times, I ended up knowing them all by heart! The entire process was mind-numbing.

(My guess is that the real intent behind this bureaucratic ordeal is that callers will hang up, forego the purpose of their call, and learn to live without their questions being answered or their problems resolved, despite being assured that their call was important and that customer satisfaction a priority!)

But, praise God, we have direct access to the throne of grace thanks to the mediating atonement of our Lord and Savior Jesus Christ. Not only do we have free access to the Father because of our Advocate who sits at His right hand, we are instructed to pray using

His name when we do. Moreover, we have a Comforter and Counselor who knows our groanings better than we do and prays on our behalf. Even when, in His good pleasure, God delays responding (thereby working patience in us), our waiting on the Lord is *never* in vain. He who answers our call is not some impersonal representative, ill-equipped to handle our particular need. As we're told in Isaiah 40:31,

> *But they that wait upon the LORD shall renew their strength; they shall mount up with wings as eagles; they shall run, and not be weary; and they shall walk, and not faint.*

# 29

# As Unto the Lord

EXCELLENCE is a word that is thrown around quite readily these days. Yet, like so many other words in our vocabulary, it has lost much of its punch because of the all-too-many counterfeits posing as the real thing. Likewise, there are too many examples in daily life that constitute assaults on excellence. Just visit your local mall and you will discover how difficult it is to find someone who works at a store, let alone someone to help you. And then there are those instances when you call in to your insurance company, bank, or technical support plan, and the "helpful" automated voice operator directs you to punch a series of numbers on your phone, which often ends up at a dead-end or a prompt that alerts you that the mailbox you wish to reach is full! Whatever happened to customer service?

One need not look too far from the pages of the Bible to discover that, rather than living out the idea that those who wish to be great should serve others, our culture has deteriorated into a mindset that seeks to get the greatest possible gain from the least amount of (and often slipshod) effort. Whatever happened to doing all things excellently *as unto the Lord*?

Proverbs 22:29 reads: *You see a man skillful at his work? He shall enter the service of kings, not the service of obscure men.*

The word *skillful* can also be translated as diligent. In other words, those who do what they are supposed to do, the way it is supposed to be done, and do so to the best of their abilities, are those who will be rewarded with the greatest opportunities.

Homeschooling parents have the utmost occasion and context to make this concept a hallmark of their children's education. It is not that Christian schools can't emphasize excellence; they most certainly can and in many cases do. However, the one-on-one attention a homeschooling parent/teacher can direct to her students not only enables excellence to be stressed, but also to be attained. This close-up and personal concentration allows for the Biblical standard of excellence to be applied without the constraints of a regular classroom setting.

Just because the current humanistic, academic models say that 70 percent of something constitutes a passing grade is no reason for a homeschool to accept such a substandard. Does anyone reading this really want to be operated on by a surgeon who only learned 70 percent of what was being taught while in medical school or during his internship? When the emphasis is not serving before kings, then *how good, good enough is* becomes a currency that can be inflated and devalued. A good, Biblical answer is in order: *As unto the Lord.*

Rather than codify what this means in every imaginable situation, I will give you an example from my own experience. I've always asked my students (my own children and others I've tutored or taught) to present me with only their best work. How did I define best work? Simply put, I instructed them to submit an assignment that they had worked and reworked until they felt there was nothing more that they could add or delete to improve it. Anything less wasn't their best work. If our standard is 100 percent in all we do, any grade we get that is less than what we want will reflect areas needing improvement, rather than be evidence of halfhearted, apathetic efforts.

Proverbs 22:29 speaks of earthly kings and people of influence. But, lest we forget, our primary audience in all we do, think, and say is the triune God of Scripture, in whose presence we all will stand for judgment.

*For God shall bring every work into judgment, with every secret thing, whether it be good, or whether it be evil.* (Ecclesiastes 12:14)

# 30

# You Get What You Expect

Oh that children would stay little! That is the lament I used to hear over and over as relatives or friends who hadn't seen my children for some time commented on how much they had grown. The "enjoy them now" perspective indicated that there would be a time when I wouldn't be enjoying them all that much.

Is this a twentieth to twenty-first century cultural thing, or is it something that the Scripture tells us to expect? Is the normal and expected condition realized by parents and their older children (say fifteen and up) one of conflict over what is right and what is wrong? Should we gear up for these stressful battles the way we anticipate the removal of wisdom teeth? Is it a given that children will reject the teachings of their parents?

I guess it boils down to *you get what you expect*. If you *expect* your children to rebel and challenge the standards you've established as the for-me-and-my-house rules, then I submit that any defiance on the part of your children will be considered normal rather than abnormal. After all, isn't this the message we get from all the "experts" and people in the know? Don't teenagers need to be approached on their own wavelength with their own music and culture and their own identities? Are defiance and rejection of

God's law inevitable? Is this how the Scripture instructs us to view these matters?

I submit that the Word of God is quite clear that parents need to continually and repeatedly lay out God's standards for living (His commandments) and continually and repeatedly demonstrate the application of them to the lives of their children. In the process, sin needs to be identified for what it is: a failure to do those things commanded in Scripture or doing those things that the Scripture prohibits. The desire to be "nice" or lenient on the part of the parents needs to be viewed for what it is—disobedience to God's clear commands to train up children in the way they should go. This most certainly includes, although it is not limited to, providing a thoroughly Christian education.

For those parents who were raised outside the context of a covenant household and who came to faith as adults (like me), the initial step in being able to help steward the lives of your children involves reevaluating all that you think and have learned through the lens of the Bible. I began such a trek twenty-two years ago when I had the benefit of being mentored from a perspective that began with the authority and sufficiency of the Word of God and never wavered from it. As a result of reading, digesting, and applying the material in Rushdoony's works, such as his Biblical law trilogy, his systematic theology, and his material on Christian education, coupled with the opportunity to have one-on-one contact with him and his wife, I have been able to withstand the darts of the enemy while receiving the correction that the Word of God brings to my own life. No, this journey did not mean there were no conflicts, crises, or disagreements in my own family. Rather, Rush's teaching gave us a context to wade through the mire and confusion that were the result of sins we *all* brought to the situations of family life.

When we lose God's standard, we lose our way. If we fail to put on the *full armor of God*, we will be defeated at every turn. Parents, we have been entrusted with a very important responsibility and charge: to bring up our children in the nurture and admonition of the Lord. When we equip ourselves to do this faithfully, we are in a position to provide the kind of hands-on training and guidance that will understand the nature of rebellion, but at the same time, give it no quarter.

# TEACHING CURRICULUM

# 31

## Some Funny Things Happen on the Way to Homeschooling

One of the mistakes that is commonly made in a homeschool setting is to assume that all children will learn the same way or at the same pace. Additionally, not all curriculum choices will work equally well for all students. It is important to figure out your children's learning styles and then find books and materials that will ensure the best possible learning experience. Hand-me-downs aren't a bad thing, so long as when it comes to using them, they fit.

I have homeschooled my three children, all with different orientations to learning. The flexibility that homeschooling allowed made it so I could encourage them to independently explore subjects that strongly interested them (literature, history, etc.), while being able to be more hands-on with those subjects that proved difficult and uninviting. By the time I came to my third student, I had plenty of curriculum on hand and was ready to go. But, I discovered that much of what had accumulated and had worked so well for my older two, just wasn't a good fit for her. It was then that I made my greatest improvements as a teacher, by finding innovative ways to bring about understanding and explain the relevance of what she was studying.

I won't lie to you: sometimes this can be frustrating and downright difficult. But that's never been a good reason to quit at anything worthwhile. I've had many opportunities to praise God for giving me insight as to how to "unlock" the door to understanding.

## Child #1

The first real challenge in his academic life occurred with fractions. For some reason, this concept completely eluded him. That is, until I put a dollar sign in front of any math problem he faced. He was always eager to have and earn money, so this proved a surefire way to keep him involved. All I needed to do was put the question in terms of money, and what had previously been an obstacle became an area he looked forward to, and often wanted to tackle first each school day.

## Child #3

This one had a hard time with numbers early on. The question *What is 13 minus 3?* would stump her. It didn't seem to help to use pencils, or paper clips, or other physical objects to communicate the concept of subtraction. Finally I got creative and made use of the fact that she had been golfing since she was three years old. When I posed the question like this: *Let's say you are on hole #3 and Daddy is on hole #13. How many holes will it take you to catch up with him?* The answer "10" was out of her mouth almost before I finished asking my question. After that, I would tell her to think in golf terms.

But there are upsides to struggling students. Sometimes they come up with creative explanations for their setbacks. The daughter whose favorite subject is NOT math is now working on algebraic word problems. She often comes up with some great one-liners. For example, we recently had this interchange during an algebra lesson. The problem stated:

> *Let's say your brother has been visiting you for the weekend from college. Five minutes after he leaves to go back to college, you discover that he forgot his books. So you get in your car and drive to catch up to him. If your average speed is 10 mph faster than your brother's speed, and you catch him in 25 minutes, how fast did you drive?*

My student didn't waste any time with this one. "Hasn't anyone ever heard of cell phones!" In her mind, the problem did not qualify as a real problem. "I would just call him and tell him to get his own books!"

## Child #2

This child (now about to start law school) demonstrated early on her proclivity for persuading a jury. She had just received a grade of 37 percent on her fourth grade science test. I pointed out that she hadn't prepared very well, leaving many answers blank. She immediately challenged my grade and told me she should be eligible for partial credit. "Really?" I retorted. "And how do you figure that?" She replied without even stopping for a breath, "I should get partial credit for the ones I left blank. That showed I *knew* I didn't know the answer!"

Home teaching moms, don't despair when one of your students struggles. It will serve as a character building experience for him and the opportunity for you to become a better teacher. And, you might get some good laughs along the way!

# 32

# SETTING GOALS

I have always liked the idea of setting homeschooling goals around the time of the New Year rather than just at the beginning of the school year in September. It gives us a chance to tweak our earlier decisions and make necessary scheduling revisions where indicated, and adjust our priorities. We're in the process of doing just that with our homeschooled student in a number of areas: discipleship, academics, athletics, and other spheres of personal and spiritual growth.

Giving focused attention to these areas gives us a better chance of realizing success. Additionally, it allows us to reassign proper accountability to our daughter in working out the plan that she has helped to formulate. By outlining those things that are important to her, she is establishing a blueprint for her time and resource allocation. Of course, without submission to the King of kings and Lord of lords according to His Word, our efforts are futile and destined to burnout or eventual failure.

# 33

# REDEEMING THE TIME

Whether you are homeschooling one child or a number of them, it is important for the homeschooling parent/teacher to use her time and her children's time wisely. There are some basic principles that will help make the homeschool experience a more successful and productive one.

1. Have a designated place where teaching takes place and a separate space where your student(s) can do independent work.

2. Get Caller ID and an answering machine so that you can decide which calls to take and those to ignore.

3. If you are interrupted, have your students be prepared to switch to "independent work" until you are ready to resume working with them. These could include reading, musical instrument practice, finishing up a previous assignment, or going ahead in the lesson independently. Being prepared for these inevitable times (e.g., having to schedule a repair visit for an impaired washing machine) makes it so your student is not sitting idly waiting for your return.

4. When you are driving to sport activities or doctor's appointments, have a tape or CD series that you listen to only in the car. (We've listened to history tapes, biographies, and sermons while driving on short and extended trips at what I

call our auto university.) You can also use car trips to have your student read aloud and discuss a lesson or assignment.

5. Make use of the various activities of the family and turn them into educational lessons. Visits to the vet and pediatrician can give your students a chance to get questions answered and see how these professionals conduct their business. Make sure your students are always ready to "grab some reading material" for stints in the waiting room. Better to have them get some schoolwork done than just browse through mindless magazines.

6. Be ready to have to change plans on short notice. Sometimes a great opportunity will arise that requires you to alter your schedule for the day. A free ticket to a show or museum and/or an unexpected visit from a relative or family friend is a good reason to reschedule academics to later in the evening or the weekend.

Homeschooling is different than day school and some advance planning can allow for learning to take place in many ways and venues. I'm sure there are plenty of other sound practices that are implemented every day by homeschooling moms across the country. Feel free to share some.

# 34

# PUBLIC SPEAKING
# AND LEADERSHIP

A friend of mine, who happens to be a lawyer, told me years ago
that if he had to do it all over again, he would have spent
much more time in speech, debate, or drama classes. His reason
was simple: lawyers who are well accustomed to speaking publicly
are much more at ease in trial situations. Others who didn't work
on their public speaking skills from an early age were more apt to
push papers or have to settle cases out of court.

I've noticed over the years that those of us who are willing to
get up and speak in front of an audience (either small or large) are
more apt to be those in leadership positions. I've always been surprised at how many folks find speaking in front of a group intimi-
dating.

For the reasons stated above, I have made public speaking a
focal point in my homeschool curriculum. From the time my children were young, they were memorizing large portions of Scripture. By the time my son was about seven years old, he had
memorized the first six chapters of the book of Proverbs. He would
compete in homeschool fairs in recitation competitions and eventually competed in speech contests. My daughters have, from the
time they were quite young, performed in front of audiences of various sizes. The pieces I selected for them to present inspired and

encouraged those in their audience. This was not so that mama and papa could show off our little darlings. No, it was practice for the leadership roles we wanted them to assume as they got older.

My advice to parents is to NOT underestimate the ability of their children to memorize lengthy pieces and present them dramatically—in other words with an understanding of what they are reciting. Even if parents find they aren't capable themselves, they should NOT prejudge their own children's abilities. Take a stab at it and find out just how amazing your young children are.

# 35

# INCENTIVES

Many times during my tenure as a home educating parent, I've run into the situation where my child just wasn't "getting" a particular subject, despite the fact that I had good curriculum, a good personal grasp of the material, and had attempted many different approaches to the subject matter. More than once I almost succumbed to the idea that I just wasn't qualified to deal with this learning issue. I thought that maybe an "expert" needed to be called in. So, I'd make phone calls and talk to those who taught professionally. I soon discovered that they didn't have any easy fixes or answers. In fact, much of their advice included avenues I had already explored, and they were impressed with things I had tried that they'd never considered. But before too long, I had a breakthrough that enabled me to help my students over seemingly impossible hurdles.

Scripture tells us that the worker is worthy of his hire. I have applied this principle in my homeschool by *incentivizing* subject areas in which I want to see positive results. No, I'm not talking about bribery. I'm talking about demonstrating to my children that I'm willing to reward them for accomplishing a significant task and that there is an immediate good reason for them to try harder.

Let me give some illustrations:

Each of my children has been expected to learn the Westminster Shorter Catechism. We used it as opportunity for writing drills and memorization work. When my son was in high school, I taught church history at a homeschool co-op. I put a sizable chunk of prize money up for first, second, and third place for a "catechism bee." In the process, my students learned the essential doctrines of the faith and got to pocket some cash at the same time.

When my youngest was learning to read, she would often get frustrated and want to abandon our phonics lesson. I needed to incentivize this subject area. I used stickers and stars, but realized quickly that she could take or leave this reward and would still want to give up. So, I did a little research and found out that she really wanted a "grown-up" golf bag like her sister had. I promised her that whenever she reached lesson sixty and could read any page prior without a mistake, she would earn her bag. It didn't happen overnight, but she was committed to the activity and was toting a "real bag" just like *the big girls carried* before too long.

Many times when I'm out with my youngest as she's practicing golf, I can see that the routine is becoming monotonous. I often put up a challenge such as, "If you can hit that barrel out at one hundred yards, I'll let you decide what we have for dinner tonight." Suddenly, her focus gets very pronounced and she's working at winning this contest. Keep in mind that it isn't an easy task I've laid before her. But, as she pursues it, she's honing her skills and improving her results. Often, bystanders and spectators marvel at what they interpret as her desire for perfection. When I inform them what the reward is, they scratch their heads finding it hard to believe that someone would work that hard for such an inconsequential reward.

As children get older, the nature of the incentive needs to change as what thrills one child often leaves another cold. So, the rewards need to be tailored to the individual and need not be expensive—just creative. Before too long, the student's personal desire for excellence kicks in (whether in academics, athletics, or the arts) and he begins to create internal, personal incentives in the specific endeavor.

# 36

# COMBATING THE
# HUMANISTIC INQUISITION

My daughter and I are currently in the midst of a study of idolatry. Sound funny? Well, since one of the major themes of the Bible is to abstain from worshipping idols, it is incumbent upon me, the Christian homeschool teacher, to make sure that the subject is thoroughly covered and properly understood. Unfortunately, most parents spend more time on "Look both ways before crossing the street" and "Have you cleaned your room?" than giving their children a strong foundational understanding of this topic. Since the first two of the Ten Commandments deal with idolatry, and do so in very strong language, it is a subject that should not be taken lightly.

We are currently going through the second volume of the *Institutes of Biblical Law* by R. J. Rushdoony. We read a chapter a day and discuss it together. Sometimes the discussions are so far-reaching that an hour and a half has gone by before we realize it because we've examined the implications of a particular concept across many disciplines.

A recent chapter dealt with idolatry and the law. Dr. Rushdoony has many insightful points. For example, he describes the dedicated assault on Christianity in our culture as the *Humanist Inquisition* in action, because the humanistic state won't tolerate dissent from its stated theological position and persecutes those who deviate from it. No wonder Christian homeschoolers are often in the bull's-eye of state and federal legislators and regulators who try to gain access and control over those they wish to proselytize.

Later in the chapter, Dr. Rushdoony makes the following statement, having previously expounded on the Biblical definition of idolatry and its manifestations:

> All who are content with a humanistic law system and do not strive to replace it with Biblical law are guilty of idolatry. They have forsaken the covenant of their God, and they are asking us to serve other gods. They are thus idolaters, and are, in our generation, when our world is idolatrous and our states also, to be objects of missionary activity. They must be called out of their idolatry into the service of the living God. (p. 468)

For those who have already taken the obedient step of teaching and nurturing their children in terms of God's Word, this perspective is probably not new to you. However, its implications are enormous. Among other things, it means that it is time for homeschooling families to stop apologizing for their decisions to obey God, feeling the need to justify their course of action to those who have chosen the path of compromise. It is time to stand firm on God's command to make disciples of ALL nations, starting with our own families. Quoting Rushdoony again:

> It is our duty to evangelize, to work for the conversion of men and nations to Christ as Lord and Savior. At the same time, as part of our evangelism, we witness to the meaning of covenant law, and, in our own personal dealings, we live by it: we practice the tithe, restitution, debt-free living, and much, much more. Only as God's law is made the practice of man can it become the practice of nations. Only those laws are enforceable which virtually all men are already enforcing in their own lives. (p. 468)

Therefore, among the greatest tools of evangelism remains our faithful application of God's law-word to every area of life and thought. When we do so, we are acting as a beacon of light to a dark and hopeless world and are boldly manifesting the position that, "As for me and my house, we will serve the Lord." What better way to combat those who seek to destroy our faith, our families, and our foundations.

# 37

# WHY WRITE?

I am repeatedly asked for my advice regarding how to teach writing to grammar-school age children. Not only have I taught my own children how to write, but I have taught in co-op settings and privately tutored other homeschooled students. To fully answer the question, I will begin by repeating my opening remarks to each class or initial one-on-one tutoring session I've ever taught. Here goes:

There are four kinds of people:

Those who have *something of value* to say and *say it well.*

Those who have *something of value* to say and *say it poorly.*

Those who have *nothing of value* to say and *say it well.*

Those who have *nothing of value* to say and *say it poorly.*

I then let my students know that I have no interest in helping people who have nothing of value to say. From my point of view if they have nothing of value to say, I certainly don't want to help them say it better—whichever category (three or four) they fall into.

What do I mean by something of value to say? Simply put, the gospel of Jesus Christ is the most valuable piece of information that can be imparted. Admittedly, not everything one is called to write will include the gospel message, but ultimately, those with a Biblical worldview, who understand that the law-word of God speaks to every area of life and thought, are those who have *something of value* to say. By implication, this means that if someone is going to communicate (*either orally or by the written word*), *what* they have to say, *how* they say it, *why* they say it, and *when* and *where* they choose to say it are all relevant questions needing to be answered.

Now, back to the question of teaching writing. As children learn to read phonetically, writing out the words they learn and saying them aloud cements new words into their vocabulary. Likewise, as they are provided with challenging and worthwhile reading material, their vocabulary will increase. It is my opinion that young grammar-school age children should spend the majority of their time acquiring knowledge by being given a steady diet of "nutritious" books with ideas meant to stretch their understanding of the world in which God has placed them. In essence, this is increasing their arsenal of having *something of value* to say.

Initially, evidence of concepts and ideas being absorbed will come in the form of comments, questions, or discussion. It is only when someone has something of value to say that being able to articulate those ideas with the written word makes any sense at all. Otherwise, it just becomes an exercise in putting words on paper without the intent to communicate something of value. The home-schooling parent can assist by acting as a secretary taking dictation—writing what the child says orally—thereby helping the child see that writing is merely taking what one says and committing it to paper. Then, the parent can interject suggestions by applying the rules of grammar and syntax in order to have the child's ideas put forth in a clearer and more coherent fashion. This helps the child see that writing is just another way to communicate. Once the parent has completed the dictation and suggested rephrasing and grammatical corrections, the child should take the paper and prepare a final copy in his best handwriting. Now he has produced something worth reading, and you should seek a greater audience for it than just you and your child.

A couple of things will become apparent with this exercise: good writing takes effort, practice, and time. Finding the correct words (*a dictionary or thesaurus helps*) and arranging them in such a way as to make their meaning clear is an activity that in the end produces a product worthy of someone's attention and time investment.

No one who enjoys talking should hate writing. If a child has been taught that he has been put in this world to glorify God and enjoy Him forever (*answer to the first question of the Westminster Shorter Catechism*), and additionally knows that he has been privileged to take part in the *Great Commission* to share the good news of Jesus Christ with those he comes in contact, it follows that he should strive to fulfill that commission the best way possible. Writing will then be an opportunity to let others know what he believes, rather than just an assignment that has to get done.

If you find that your child has difficulty with dictating to you (*can't really think of anything to say on any topic*), then I suggest you have him copy portions of good literature or Bible passages as a way to train his ear how to write well. Afterwards, you can dictate the portion or passage back to him and have him write it as you say it. This process helps create a pathway that enables the student to realize that writing is what the authors of his favorite books did in order for him to have the opportunity to receive and appreciate their ideas.

There are many opportunities in life for kids to write: letters to family and friends, "reviews" of books or movies they've enjoyed, and summaries of topics learned in history or literature. Or, for those who need a little more incentive: if your student seeks permission to buy something or go somewhere, inform him that he needs to put the request in writing in a clear manner before you will even entertain the idea at all. This might spur a reluctant writer to overcome the hurdles to acquire a greater proficiency in persuasive writing, in order to get what he wants!

The homeschooling teacher need not stress over this process. Some children will take to this sooner than others. It's like walking and potty training: we care more *that* it happens rather than *when* it happens, just so long as it *eventually* happens. The important part is to continually provide material that enables your student to have more to talk and think about. Help him get to the point where he knows he is able to bring ideas and opinions to the conversations of life—*something of value* to say, and with your help, the ability to *say it well.*

# CURRICULUM

# 38

## BUILDING A HOMESCHOOL LENDING LIBRARY

Over the years I have used a wide variety of curricula and audio/video resources to help me in the home education of my children. Some of these were used by all three children; others were acquired to suit the particular needs of one child's individual learning style. In the process, I was building quite a good library and a body of knowledge of the various publishers. Then, I began to purchase resources (both new and used) that I felt would be helpful to me to further educate myself to be the best teacher possible for my kids. In time, I needed more and more bookcases to house what would become useful tools for my own children, those I tutored or taught, and eventually to become part of our homeschool lending library. This has been a great outreach for my family as the library continues to loan out materials for review or a year's worth of use to new homeschoolers and veterans alike.

Homeschool families, co-ops, and homeschool-friendly churches should make a concerted effort to establish libraries to serve their local cities and communities. With the increasing number of families making the choice to provide a distinctively Christian education to their children, being ready to help is a very proactive and godly endeavor.

Our library required families to sign up to participate and fill out a lending agreement. It included the following:

There is no fee to borrow materials. However, library materials undergo normal wear and tear, so we encourage donations to help us replace worn-out materials and to expand the library.

Lending period is for two weeks unless special arrangements are made.

Books and other materials are to be returned in the condition they are received.

In the event library materials are not returned in usable condition, we require that the borrower pay replacement costs in addition to a service fee of $10.

Any problem with library materials should be brought to our attention immediately.

Materials are lent to you and your family and should not be lent to other individuals or families. If other families wish to borrow materials, they need to fill out an agreement in order to borrow directly from us.

It is the responsibility of the borrower to return library materials as agreed and not the responsibility of the library to call and pick them up. However, convenient arrangements can be made for pickup and delivery.

Lending privileges may be revoked at the discretion of the library staff.

Since we are now expanding the lending privileges, other conditions may be added to this agreement as experience dictates. In that case, you will be notified in writing of such changes, if and when they occur.

# 39

# Homeschooling Through High School

Frequently Asked Questions:

## *Why would I want to homeschool through high school?*

The book of Proverbs stresses the importance of wisdom, knowledge, and discretion. Throughout a young person's life, it is important that the primary influences be godly individuals who know the young person's strengths and weaknesses and can provide hands-on support in helping him maneuver through the many deceptions and lures of our modern humanistic culture. Homeschooling provides such a situation.

## *Aren't high school subjects harder to teach?*

That depends. With a myriad of curriculum choices available (complete with teacher's editions and answer keys) much of the learning experience can be tailored to meet individual academic needs. Many families make use of co-ops where parents divide up subject matter according to their area of expertise or experience.

*What about athletic opportunities and activities?*

A number of private Christian schools allow homeschooled students to participate in athletic activities. Also, drama, speech, and other programs may be available, either through a school or by way of a homeschooling co-op. Of course, if there is something that parents want that doesn't exist, they can always start a project themselves!

*What about socialization?*

This is a nonissue. In our current society, no one who attends church, goes to the grocery store, or is involved with extended family has any difficulty in socializing if they have been taught the rules of godly living from the time they were little. The entire socialization issue is a humanistic construct. Surely we can't say that the students who are graduates of public school settings are systematically socialized in ways that most people would consider positive.

*Will homeschooling through high school hamper my child's chances of getting into college?*

Not according to the experience of homeschooling families around the country. Many have attained very high SAT/ACT scores. Moreover, many college professors actually prefer home-school graduates because they tend to be self-starters and ready for serious self-disciplined study. It is not unusual for homeschooled graduates to finish college in less than four years.

*What should I be looking to achieve in my homeschool?*

The most important result of successful homeschooling will be the production of godly individuals who look to the Word of God to provide a perspective and standard for what is right and true and honorable. With this orientation, all areas of life and thought can be groomed and educated to the glory of God.

*Can I tailor educational opportunities for my high-school age child?*

Most definitely. The major advantage of homeschooling is that it allows you to spend extra time on those areas that need more personalized attention. Moreover, if your student has special gifts or talents, the flexibility of the schedule allows for greater concentration on the pursuit of excellence in that particular area.

*How will I evaluate our progress?*

Many homeschool publishers include tests as part of their curriculum choices. Standardized tests are available to monitor progress. However, the best indication of how well a student is learning is not in the answers they give, but in the questions they ask.

*Are there people to help me as I get started?*

Yes, there are a multitude of resources. A good place to start is Home School Legal Defense Association (www.hslda.org). Spending time at this website will give you many resources to check out and many links to pursue.

*Where can I go for instruction as to how to be a good teacher?*

There are a number of good resources for this. Much can be accomplished by making use of the teacher editions and guides that come with many courses. There are many homeschooling magazines and websites and support groups that offer seminars and newsletters to help you.

*What resources are available?*

Go to the Internet and type in homeschooling and you will have many days of reading material. Videos are also available, as are books that can be found online and at many Christian bookstores and booksellers.

*What are my options in setting a course of study?*

Depending on what your student is interested in pursuing, you can make use of online courses, community college courses, DVD courses, audio CD courses, and many computer-based ones. If your school will be college prep, you can find out what requirements have to be met (subjects covered) and tailor your curriculum accordingly.

*Where does a Biblical worldview enter the picture when it comes to homeschooling through high school?*

This is probably the most important question. Since there is no neutrality when in comes to ethics and morality, it is vital that a Biblical worldview is presented in every subject taught. Jesus Christ *is* the Way, the Truth, and the Life, and His law-word must be the standard by which all areas of life and thought are judged. Browsing through the offerings at www.ChalcedonStore.com is a good place to find helpful materials and resources.

# 40

# CATEGORIES

People often homeschool because they desire to provide their children with a distinctively Christian education. This is a good thing. Although proper curriculum and a balanced schedule are a big piece of the puzzle, parents often fail to pay enough attention to girding themselves with a strong theological and philosophical base. Consequently, they may overlook areas or subjects in their own background and experience that aren't Biblical in orientation. It is important to reevaluate the categories in which you think, ensuring that they are Biblical categories and not humanistic ones.

Let me give you an example. This past week I purchased a supplemental biology program called *Biology 101: Biology According to the Days of Creation*. Here is a brief description:

> *Biology 101* is a complete overview of the world of biology from a Biblical perspective, in a set of 4 DVDs. Their short film "From Genesis to Genes" was the first-place winner in the "Creation Category" at the *2004 San Antonio Independent Christian Film Festival*, sponsored by Vision Forum Ministries. The film generated a lot of excitement at the Festival, and their much-anticipated full version (over 4 hours) is now available, entitled "Biology 101."

Taking God's word as the starting point, this DVD course divides all life according to the days of creation. An exciting, visually rich experience, it is designed specifically for ages 15 years old and up. Filmed in locations throughout America's beautiful Northwest, *Biology 101* is full of accurate and fascinating information supported by hundreds of captivating visuals and graphics. The 4 DVD set is accompanied by a printable (pdf) guidebook, allowing the student to easily review all the information covered in the film. Each guidebook segment includes a multiple choice quiz and discussion questions. A 12-page "Course Accreditation Program" booklet is included for those families who want a year-long biology course.

*Biology 101* was developed and hosted by Wes Olson, Multnomah Bible College graduate, veteran filmmaker of 15 years, and homeschooling father. Wes guides you through the world of "biological science," unraveling and decoding terms and ideas. This DVD course of study will help you fully integrate the world of biology into an accurate Biblical worldview.

This new program challenged and corrected me in the very first segment. Keep in mind that I've been homeschooling for twenty-five years and have never embraced the evolutionary mindset in teaching science; yet, this product quickly unearthed a premise I hadn't challenged in all those years. Simply put, it is erroneous to classify human beings in the same taxonomic "kingdom" as the animals. By subconsciously accepting this, I had given credence to the false teaching man is just an "advanced" animal. In teaching my older two children, I never fully challenged the taxonomic classification that I had been taught during my years in school. Genesis clearly states that man is categorically different from the animals, however similar some structures may be. I had failed to filter biological classifications through the lens of Scripture.

Homeschooling parents should make a concentrated effort to examine ALL the presuppositions that they hold in all areas to see if they inadvertently hold a view that doesn't have agreement with the Holy Word of God. Not sure where to start? Well, Chalcedon's materials, including its bimonthly magazine *Faith for All of Life* is a good place to start, as are the Biblical worldview materials from *American Vision* and *Vision Forum*.

Don't put off or abandon homeschooling until you are totally in line with the Bible in all areas. Learn alongside your children, and take advantage of the head start you have on them, as you organize their education in a *categorically* Biblical fashion. As Proverbs 3:5–6 promises:

> *Trust in the LORD with all your heart;*
> *And lean not on your own understanding.*
> *In all your ways acknowledge him,*
> *and He shall direct your paths.*

# 41

# A Happy Alliance

Rousas John Rushdoony was a strong voice in the twentieth century for Christian education. He made himself available as an expert witness in court cases to Christian schools and homeschooling families alike when attempts were made to usurp the primary role of parents in the education of their children. That is why Rushdoony is often referred to as the *father* of the Christian school and homeschooling movements.

Note that he receives credit for fathering *both* movements. Good fathers delight when their children cooperate and act supportively of one another. Likewise, the Chalcedon Foundation, with its *faith for all of life* message, is eager for these two orientations to Christian education to promote and encourage each other, as its founder envisioned.

An important aspect of this cooperation does *not* involve one trying to remake the other in its own image. In so many ways, the Christian day school and the homeschool need to operate differently. However, rather than viewing each other as competing entities, deliberate teamwork can provide a much more productive and scriptural means by which to support and further their mutually shared goals.

Two years ago, I was asked by a newly formed Christian junior and senior high school to sit on their board of directors. At first, even I was surprised—a homeschooling mother sitting on the board of a day school? Very quickly I could see the Lord's hand in this offer and, with my husband's approval, accepted it. Since my passion has been and continues to be the Christian education of Christian youth, lending my talents and efforts to the school was consistent with this calling.

So, here's my challenge. If you are a homeschooling family, find ways that you can participate and support Christian schools in your locale that are faithful to the Word of God and self-consciously teach their students to do the same. If you are part of a Christian school, encourage the participation in athletics, the arts, and even some elective classes for homeschooling families—offered at times they will be likely to attend and at a cost they are likely to be able to afford. And, on a bigger scale, what if someone with an abundance of God-given resources were to set up regional centers where joint activities in athletics, drama, and music were accessible to both small Christian schools and homeschoolers alike? Maybe that would act as an effective magnet drawing those interested in providing a Christian education for their children to "check out" what Christian education is all about. To quote a line from a well-known baseball movie, "If we build it, they will come!"

I'm thinking that maybe they will! What do you think?

# 42

# Recruiting Your Homeschool Faculty

I'm sure you are thinking that I made a mistake in my title. You're saying to yourself, *I thought homeschooling was about parents teaching their children.*

Over my twenty-five years as a home educator, I have been the primary teacher for my children/students. Having had the benefit of a good private school education myself, I have been able to handle the subjects of English grammar, mathematics, and history quite well. However, there were subjects (specifically foreign language, science, and music) that I was not as proficient in, although I had received good grades when I was in school. In those cases, I delegated my teaching responsibilities to other people, either through private lessons or co-op group settings.

With each successive child, I've improved upon my methods and streamlined the process. I have gotten rid of much of the "busy work" assignments that some textbooks recommend, knowing that they were often there for the teacher handling twenty plus students. Since I didn't have that situation, I had the luxury of making my assignments interesting or, at least, practical. However, one-on-one with Mom could and did sometimes become tedious both from the teacher's and the student's perspectives. In order to combat this, I "got creative" and found a variety of sources to supplement my teaching.

There are a number of publishers that cater to home schools and produce DVDs and CD-ROM courses for the computer. With the current technology available, it is very possible to get an entire faculty of excellent teachers to work with your students, right from your own television set. The fact that the presentations can be viewed repeatedly, if need be, coupled with the fact that the production values are usually quite good, makes this learning environment one that surpasses many fine academic institutions. Some publishers even allow you to call and get assistance with any portion of the subject that is not understood. We have used this method for chemistry, algebra, general science, biology, world history, American history, physics, anatomy and physiology, Spanish, Shakespeare's plays, geometry, and English literature. To be sure, not all of these resources come from a self-conscious Christian perspective, but many aren't inconsistent with our faith. And, with those that spout the "religion of evolution," the pause button is liberally used for me to clarify and/or instruct on particular points.

My children look back fondly on many of these teachers as though they had actually physically been in the same classroom with them. An interesting aside: when my youngest, (who had the benefit of watching some of these courses alongside her older sister of seven years), took these courses herself, she remembered so much in detail that she could often say what the instructor was going to say before he even said it!

For those whose budgets make it difficult to purchase all these series for your own personal library, I recommend that families consider purchasing and sharing with other homeschoolers. Or better yet, see if you can get your church or co-op to invest in a lending library so that homeschooling families can make use of these materials. A regular monthly subscription fee could purchase a considerable amount. And, of course, you can make use of eBay and HSLDA's resale sites to save some dollars as you do. I think you will find this is an excellent way to broaden the scope of your homeschool.

# CONCLUSION

# 43

## PREPARING FOR SCHOOL:
### HOMESCHOOL OR CHRISTIAN ACADEMY?

Worldviews are like belly buttons—everybody has one. However, if one is truly viewing the world from a Christian perspective (a Christian/Biblical worldview), then every area of life and thought needs to be filtered through the lens of God's Word. This is not a weekend undertaking capable of being crammed into someone's spare time. Nor will you likely find reading *A Biblical Worldview for Dummies* particularly gratifying. No, short gimmicks or patches won't do the trick.

The answer is immersion. Saturate your children, in all subjects and activities, with Scripture as the foundation and faith in Jesus Christ as the impetus and object of the undertaking. That's how parents can hope to inculcate a Christian world and life view in their children.

So, the question becomes, where is the best place to achieve this goal? Certainly not in the state education system or secular private schools. However academically elite these may seem, they are specifically geared NOT to impart a practical Christianity, proclaiming the faith for all of life. The Christian academy is a good choice for parents whose background, circumstance, or inclination makes homeschooling unrealistic or unworkable. However, this option involves more, not less, work on the part of the parents.

They need to oversee the educational process, filling in any gaps or discrepancies with a full-orbed Biblical faith. The following is a list of good questions to answer before taking this step:

What is the school's definition of education, educator, educated?

What place does the school give to parents and their preferences?

What are the priorities: Academic? Social? Character building?

What role do the teachers assume in the character building of students?

What is the school's mission statement?

What is the dress code, code of behavior?

How are infractions of rules and policies dealt with?

Is observation of classroom activities by outsiders welcome?

Is the school for Christian students or to create Christian students?

What is the view of the authority of family, church, school, state?

Is the curriculum deliberately and self-consciously Christian?

Is this school only for the college-bound student? Vocational student? To prepare for the workforce? To be ready to start a family?

Do students, parents, and teachers all give similar answers to these questions?

What is the school's philosophy of education? Is it compatible with yours?

These questions presuppose that the parents have a framework to judge the answers given. Also, careful consideration needs to be made in taking this step as you will be submitting to the authority of the school and will be directing your children (and yourselves) to respect, honor, and obey those you place in authority over them. When organized and run properly, the Christian academy is a tremendous support to the family.

Homeschooling is an option that I have exercised for the past twenty-five years and with which I have the most familiarity and practice. However, like enrolling in a day school, this option needs to be carefully planned out. Rushdoony says it well in his book *The Philosophy of the Christian Curriculum*:

The teacher who does not grow in his knowledge of his subject, in methodology and content, is a very limited teacher, and his pupils are "under-privileged" learners. (133)

The teacher as student is, above all else, a student of God's word. To be a student means to advance and grow. (134)

Our growth in teaching *requires* our growth through and under the teaching of the Holy Spirit. We must become good learners as a step towards becoming good teachers. Our profession is a very great one in Scripture: our Lord was a Teacher, and the Holy Spirit is our continuing Teacher. We cannot treat our calling lightly, nor grieve the Spirit by abusing our calling. (135)

The homeschooling parent needs to be prepared to be the source and conduit of what students need to learn, and to create a syllabus that includes subjects that demonstrate the truth of God's Word in all subject areas. Even though I used much curricula that wasn't 100 percent to my satisfaction at all times, I was able to supplement and round out important areas as a result of my own study and application of the Word of God to my life. The resources available from Chalcedon helped me tremendously and made it so that our homeschool life was consistent with our church life, our sports life, and our professional life.

In the end, it's not only about cost or logistics when choosing between homeschool and a Christian academy. It's about what is the best way to train your children to be ambassadors for the Christian world and life view. There is no more important responsibility than this one that the Lord has entrusted to us.

# Appendix

## THE MOTHER'S WAR
### BY VOX DAY

Mother's Day is, to be honest, somewhat of an annoyance. It's manifestly one of those tedious Hallmark holidays wherein everyone is supposed to run out and support the revenue stream of cardboard manufacturers in the name of expressing gratitude to mothers, fathers, grandparents and anyone else to whom we might be related.

I imagine it won't be long until September 18 is declared Anonymous Sperm Donor's Day, which will probably be celebrated by giving matching card sets to one's two mommies and lighting a candle for dear old anonymous sperm donor, whoever he might be.

Mothers are not only important, they are absolutely vital due to their position as frontline shock troops in the ongoing, centuries-long struggle for the survival of Western civilization. Despite the fact that their maternal instinct has been harassed, criticized, mocked, belittled, and subjected to a forty-year effort to indoctrinate it out of existence, our mothers stubbornly continue doing the only thing we actually need women to do in order for our civilization to survive, bearing and raising children.

We don't need female doctors. We don't need female scientists. We don't need female entrepreneurs. We don't need female producers of PowerPoint presentations. And we really don't need female politicians.

While we can argue about whether such luxuries are beneficial or detrimental to society, there is no arguing the empirical evidence which proves that civilization has survived without them before and could easily do so again.

But without mothers, there is no civilization. Without mothers, there is no future for the civilized.

Europe is in the process of discovering what a world without mothers is like. It is an ugly picture, a brutal picture. It is a probable future that promises to be much worse than the most exaggerated images of past patriarchal oppression ever painted by Betty Friedan or Gloria Steinhem. Without mothers, there is only barbarism and the choice between the brothel and the burqa.

Motherhood is a sacrifice. It may mean putting off a college education and a career, or even giving them up entirely. It may mean sacrificing a flawless figure. It may mean sacrificing dreams. It definitely means putting two, three, four, or more lives ahead of your own. But motherhood is also an expression of hope. Motherhood is a vote of confidence in the future of mankind. Motherhood is the brave voice of a woman saying, "I will not live life for today. I will create life for many tomorrows."

Cards, gifts and flowers are no adequate expressions of gratitude for this living statement of faith.

In the ongoing war against Christian civilization, it is the mothers who matter most. The sterile secularists don't fear Christian intellectuals or Christian pastors, they regard the former as petty annoyances and there's little need to worry about one weekly hour of Christian teaching on Sundays overcoming forty hours of secular reprogramming from Monday to Friday. But they fear our mothers who can create children faster than they can manage to indoctrinate them. And they are downright terrified of our homeschooling mothers who rob them of their primary means of creating a new generation of secular barbarians.

Every time a woman says "I do," every time a wife turns to her husband and says "let's have another baby," every time a mother hugs her child and says "how would you like me to be your teacher?" she is striking a powerful blow in defense of her faith, her family, her church, and God. We should celebrate these bold decisions —these audacious acts—as victories, not just for the family and the faith, but for civilization and mankind.

It is not enough to thank our mothers. We owe them a debt that cannot be repaid. But we can, and we must, love them, honor them, support them and sustain them as they faithfully continue to wage their mother's war.[1]

---

1. Vox Day, "The mother's war," WorldNetDaily, May 14, 2007. Reprint permission granted.

# INDEX

# More Educational Titles From Chalcedon

### Lessons Learned From Years of Homeschooling

After nearly a quarter century of homeschooling her children, Andrea Schwartz has experienced both the accomplishments and challenges that come with being a homeschooling mom. And, she's passionate about helping you learn her most valuable lessons. Discover the potential rewards of making the world your classroom and God's Word the foundation of everything you teach. Now you can benefit directly from Andrea's years of experience and obtain helpful insights to make your homeschooling adventure God-honoring, effective, and fun.

**Paperback, 107 pages, index, $14.00**

### The Philosophy of the Christian Curriculum

By R.J. Rushdoony. The Christian School represents a break with humanistic education, but, too often, in leaving the state school, the Christian educator has carried the state's humanism with him. A curriculum is not neutral: it is either a course in humanism or training in a God-centered faith and life. The liberal arts curriculum means literally that course which trains students in the arts of freedom. This raises the key question: is freedom in and of man or Christ? The Christian art of freedom, that is, the Christian liberal arts curriculum, is emphatically not the same as the humanistic one. It is urgently necessary for Christian educators to rethink the meaning and nature of the curriculum.

**Paperback, 190 pages, index, $16.00**

### The Messianic Character of American Education

By R.J. Rushdoony. Rushdoony's study tells us an important part of American history: exactly what has public education been trying to accomplish? Before the 1830s and Horace Mann, no schools in the U.S. were state supported or state controlled. They were local, parent-teacher enterprises, supported without taxes, and taking care of all children. They were remarkably high in standard and were Christian. From Mann to the present, the state has used education to socialize the child. The school's basic purpose, according to its own philosophers, is not education in the traditional sense of the 3 R's. Instead, it is to promote "democracy" and "equality," not in their legal or civic sense, but in terms of the engineering of a socialized citizenry. Public education became the means of creating a social order of the educator's design. Such men saw themselves and the school in messianic terms. This book was instrumental in launching the Christian school and homeschool movements.

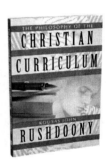

**Hardback, 410 pages, index, $20.00**

**Purchase online at www.chalcedonstore.com**

### The Victims of Dick and Jane

By Samuel L. Blumenfeld. America's most effective critic of public education shows us how America's public schools were remade by educators who used curriculum to create citizens suitable for their own vision of a utopian socialist society. This collection of essays will show you how and why America's public education declined. You will see the educator-engineered decline of reading skills. The author describes the causes for the decline and the way back to competent education methodologies that will result in a self-educated, competent, and freedom-loving populace.

**Paperback, 266 pages, index, $22.00**

### Intellectual Schizophrenia

By R.J. Rushdoony. When this brilliant and prophetic book was first published in 1961, the Christian homeschool movement was years away and even Christian day schools were hardly considered a viable educational alternative. But this book and the author's later Messianic Character of American Education were a resolute call to arms for Christian's to get their children out of the pagan public schools and provide them with a genuine Christian education. Dr. Rushdoony had predicted that the humanist system, based on anti-Christian premises of the Enlightenment, could only get worse. Rushdoony was indeed a prophet. He knew that education divorced from God and from all transcendental standards would produce the educational disaster and moral barbarism we have today. The title of this book is particularly significant in that Dr. Rushdoony was able to identify the basic contradiction that pervades a secular society that rejects God's sovereignty but still needs law and order, justice, science, and meaning to life. As Dr. Rushdoony writes, "there is no law, no society, no justice, no structure, no design, no meaning apart from God." And so, modern man has become schizophrenic because of his rebellion against God.

**Paperback, 150 pages, index, $17.00**

### Mathematics: Is God Silent?

By James Nickel. This book revolutionizes the prevailing understanding and teaching of math. The addition of this book is a must for all upper-level Christian school curricula and for college students and adults interested in math or related fields of science and religion. It will serve as a solid refutation for the claim, often made in court, that mathematics is one subject, which cannot be taught from a distinctively Biblical perspective.

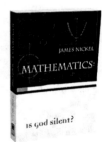

Revised and enlarged 2001 edition,
**Paperback, 408 pages, $22.00**

### The Foundations of Christian Scholarship

Edited by Gary North. These are essays developing the implications and meaning of the philosophy of Dr. Cornelius Van Til for every area of life. The chapters explore the implications of Biblical faith for a variety of disciplines.

**Paperback, 355 pages, indices, $24.00**

## Purchase online at www.chalcedonstore.com

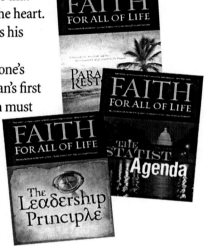

Printed in the United States
105839LV00003B/214-468/P

9 781891 375507